ECOFASCISM
REVISITED

JANET BIEHL
PETER STAUDENMAIER

ECOFASCISM REVISITED

LESSONS FROM THE GERMAN EXPERIENCE

new-compass.net

Ecofascism Revisited:
Lessons from the German Experience
2011 © by Janet Biehl and Peter Staudenmaier

First published: 1995 by AK Press

Janet Biehl's "'Ecology' and the Modernization of Fascism" (written April 1993) was originally published in *Society and Nature* 2, no. 2 (1994)

ISBN 978-82-93064-12-1
ISBN 978-82-93064-13-8 (ebook)

Published by New Compass Press
Grenmarsvegen 12,
N–3912 Porsgrunn,
Norway

Design and layout by Eirik Eiglad

new-compass.net

Contents

PREFACE

Ecofascism was originally published in 1995, at a time when American radicals were debating the place of the social question in a movement to address the ecological crisis. Would the movement recognize the centrality of the grow-or-die market economy, as well as structures of hierarchy and domination, in engendering that crisis, and affirm that ecological and social solutions must go hand in hand? Or would it disparage the social question in favor of a wilderness mystique and embrace antihumanism and Malthusianism? The German experience, it seemed to us, had much to say on these questions.

In the decade and a half since then the political landscape has shifted considerably, whether in Germany or the US or elsewhere in the world. Radical ecology movements have in some ways matured and developed more differentiated and more historically informed analyses of the ongoing ecological crisis, while predominant elements on the right castigate even the mildest forms of environmentalism as a tyrannical threat to liberty. In light of this changed context, the authors and publishers have decided to reprint our original essays in unrevised form while adding a new essay reflecting on developments since the mid-1990s. We hope that the lessons examined in this book will contribute to strengthening, informing, and invigorating a critical and confrontational ecological politics.

Janet Biehl
Peter Staudenmaier
2011

INTRODUCTION

For most compassionate and humane people today, the ecological crisis is a source of major concern. Not only do many ecological activists struggle to eliminate toxic wastes, to preserve tropical rainforests and old-growth redwoods, and to roll back the destruction of the biosphere, but many ordinary people in all walks of life are intensely concerned about the nature of the planet that their children will grow up to inhabit. In Europe as in the United States, most ecological activists think of themselves as socially progressive. That is, they also support demands of oppressed peoples for social justice and believe that the needs of human beings living in poverty, illness, warfare, and famine also require our most serious attention.

For many such people, it may come as a surprise to learn that the history of ecological politics has not always been inherently and necessarily progressive and benign. In fact, ecological ideas have a history of being distorted and placed in the service of highly regressive ends—even of fascism itself. As Peter Staudenmaier shows in the first essay in this pamphlet, important tendencies in German "ecologism," which has long roots in nineteenth-century nature mysticism, fed into the rise of Nazism in the twentieth century. During the Third Reich, Staudenmaier goes on to show, Nazi "ecologists" even made organic farming, vegetarianism, nature worship, and related themes into key elements not only in their ideology but in their governmental policies. Moreover, Nazi "ecological" ideology was used to justify the destruction of European Jewry. Yet some of the themes that Nazi ideologists articulated bear an uncomfortably close resemblance to themes familiar to ecologically concerned people today.

As social ecologists, it is not our intention to deprecate the all-important efforts that environmentalists and ecologists are making to rescue the biosphere from destruction. Quite to the contrary: It is our deepest concern to preserve the integrity of serious ecological movements from ugly reactionary tendencies that seek to exploit the widespread popular concern about ecological problems for regressive agendas. But we find that the "ecological scene" of our time—with its growing mysticism and antihumanism—poses serious problems about the direction in which the ecology movement will go.

In most Western nations in the late twentieth century, expressions of racism and anti-immigrant sentiments are not only increasingly voiced but increasingly tolerated. Equally disconcertingly, fascist ideologists and political groups are experiencing a resurgence as well. Updating their ideology and speaking the new language of ecology, these movements are once again invoking ecological themes to serve social reaction. In ways that sometimes approximate beliefs of progressive-minded ecologists, these reactionary and outright fascist ecologists emphasize the supremacy of the "Earth" over people; evoke "feelings" and intuition at the expense of reason; and uphold a crude sociobiologistic and even Malthusian biologism. Tenets of "New Age" eco-ideology that seem benign to most people in England and the United States—specifically, its mystical and antirational strains—are being intertwined with ecofascism in Germany today. Janet Biehl's essay explores this hijacking of ecology for racist, nationalistic, and fascist ends.

Taken together, these essays examine aspects of German fascism, past and present, in order to draw lessons from them for ecology movements both in Germany and elsewhere. Despite its singularities, the German experience offers a clear warning against the misuse of ecology, in a world that seems ever more willing to tolerate movements and ideologies once regarded as despicable and obsolete. Political ecology thinkers have yet to fully examine the political implications of these ideas in the English-speaking world as well as in Germany.

What prevents ecological politics from yielding reaction or fascism with an ecological patina is an ecology movement that maintains a broad social emphasis, one that places the ecological crisis in a social context. As social ecologists, we see the roots of the present ecological crisis in an irrational society—not in the biological makeup of human beings, nor

11

in a particular religion, nor in reason, science, or technology. On the contrary, we uphold the importance of reason, science, and technology in creating both a progressive ecological movement and an ecological society. It is a specific set of social relations—above all, the competitive market economy—that is presently destroying the biosphere. Mysticism and biologism, at the very least, deflect public attention away from such *social* causes. In presenting these essays, we are trying to preserve the all-important progressive and emancipatory implications of ecological politics. More than ever, an ecological commitment requires people today to avoid repeating the errors of the past, lest the ecology movement become absorbed in the mystical and antihumanistic trends that abound today.

JANET BIEHL
PETER STAUDENMAIER
1995

Peter Staudenmaier

Fascist Ecology: The "Green Wing" of the Nazi Party and its Historical Antecedents

"We recognize that separating humanity from nature, from the whole of life, leads to humankind's own destruction and to the death of nations. Only through a re-integration of humanity into the whole of nature can our people be made stronger. That is the fundamental point of the biological tasks of our age. Humankind alone is no longer the focus of thought, but rather life as a whole ... This striving toward connectedness with the totality of life, with nature itself, a nature into which we are born, this is the deepest meaning and the true essence of National Socialist thought."[1]

In our zeal to condemn the status quo, radicals often carelessly toss about epithets like "fascist" and "ecofascist," thus contributing to a sort of conceptual inflation that in no way furthers effective social critique. In such a situation, it is easy to overlook the fact that there are still virulent strains of fascism in our political culture which, however marginal, demand our attention. One of the least recognized or understood of these strains is the phenomenon one might call "actually existing ecofascism," that is, the preoccupation of authentically fascist movements with environmentalist concerns. In order to grasp the peculiar intensity and endurance of this affiliation, we would do well to examine more closely its most notorious historical incarnation, the so-called "green wing" of German National Socialism.

Despite an extensive documentary record, the subject remains an elusive one, underappreciated by professional historians and environmental activists alike. In English-speaking countries as well as in Germany itself, the very existence of a "green wing" in the Nazi movement, much less its inspiration, goals, and consequences, has yet to be adequately researched and analyzed. Most of the handful of available interpretations succumb to either an alarming intellectual affinity with their subject[2] or a naive refusal to examine the full extent of the "ideological overlap between nature conservation and National Socialism."[3] This article presents a brief and necessarily schematic overview of the ecological components of Nazism, emphasizing both their central role in Nazi ideology and their practical implementation during the Third Reich. A preliminary survey of nineteenth and twentieth century precursors to classical ecofascism should serve to illuminate the conceptual underpinnings common to all forms of reactionary ecology.

Two initial clarifications are in order. First, the terms "environmental" and "ecological" are here used more or less interchangeably to denote ideas, attitudes, and practices commonly associated with the contemporary environmental movement. This is not an anachronism; it simply indicates an interpretive approach which highlights connections to present-day concerns. Second, this approach is not meant to endorse the historiographically discredited notion that pre-1933 historical data can or should be read as "leading inexorably" to the Nazi calamity. Rather, our concern here is with discerning ideological continuities and tracing political genealogies, in an attempt to understand the past in light of our current situation—to make history relevant to the present social and ecological crisis.

The Roots of the Blood and Soil Mystique

Germany is not only the birthplace of the science of ecology and the site of Green politics' rise to prominence; it has also been home to a peculiar synthesis of naturalism and nationalism forged under the influence of the Romantic tradition's anti-Enlightenment irrationalism. Two nineteenth century figures exemplify this ominous conjunction: Ernst Moritz Arndt and Wilhelm Heinrich Riehl.

While best known in Germany for his fanatical nationalism, Arndt was also dedicated to the cause of the peasantry, which led him to a concern for the welfare of the land itself. Historians of German environmentalism mention him as the earliest example of 'ecological' thinking in the modern sense.[4] His remarkable 1815 article *On the Care and Conservation of Forests,* written at the dawn of industrialization in Central Europe, rails against shortsighted exploitation of woodlands and soil, condemning deforestation and its economic causes. At times he wrote in terms strikingly similar to those of contemporary biocentrism: "When one sees nature in a necessary connectedness and interrelationship, then all things are equally important—shrub, worm, plant, human, stone, nothing first or last, but all one single unity."[5]

Arndt's environmentalism, however, was inextricably bound up with virulently xenophobic nationalism. His eloquent and prescient appeals for ecological sensitivity were couched always in terms of the well-being of the *German* soil and the *German* people, and his repeated lunatic polemics against miscegenation, demands for Teutonic racial purity, and epithets against the French, Slavs, and Jews marked every aspect of his thought. At the very outset of the nineteenth century the deadly connection between love of land and militant racist nationalism was firmly set in place.

Riehl, a student of Arndt, further developed this sinister tradition. In some respects his 'green' streak went significantly deeper than Arndt's; presaging certain tendencies in recent environmental activism, his 1853 essay *Field and Forest* ended with a call to fight for "the rights of wilderness." But even here nationalist pathos set the tone: "We must save the forest, not only so that our ovens do not become cold in winter, but also so that the pulse of life of the people continues to beat warm and joyfully, so that Germany remains German."[6] Riehl was an implacable opponent of the rise of industrialism and urbanization; his overtly antisemitic glorification of rural peasant values and undifferentiated condemnation of modernity established him as the "founder of agrarian romanticism and anti-urbanism."[7]

These latter two fixations matured in the second half of the nineteenth century in the context of the *völkisch* movement, a powerful cultural disposition and social tendency which united ethnocentric populism with nature mysticism. At the heart of the *völkisch* temptation was a pathological response to modernity. In the face of the very real dislocations brought on by the triumph of industrial capitalism and national unification, *völkisch* thinkers preached a return to the land, to the simplicity and wholeness of a life attuned to nature's purity. The mystical effusiveness of this perverted utopianism was matched by its political vulgarity. While "the Volkish movement aspired to reconstruct the society that was sanctioned by history, rooted in nature, and in communion with the cosmic life spirit,"[8] it pointedly refused to locate the sources of alienation, rootlessness and environmental destruction in social structures, laying the blame instead to rationalism, cosmopolitanism, and urban civilization. The stand-in for all of these was the age-old object of peasant hatred and middle-class resentment: the Jews. "The Germans were in search of a mysterious wholeness that would restore them to primeval happiness, destroying the hostile milieu of urban industrial civilization that the Jewish conspiracy had foisted on them."[9]

Reformulating traditional German antisemitism into nature-friendly terms, the *völkisch* movement carried a volatile amalgam of nineteenth century cultural prejudices, Romantic obsessions with purity, and anti-Enlightenment sentiment into twentieth century political discourse. The emergence of modern ecology forged the final link in the fateful chain which bound together aggressive nationalism, mystically charged racism, and environmentalist predilections. In 1867 the German zoologist Ernst Haeckel coined the term 'ecology' and began to establish it as a scientific discipline dedicated to studying the interactions between organism and environment. Haeckel was also the chief popularizer of Darwin and evolutionary theory for the German-speaking world, and developed a peculiar sort of social darwinist philosophy he called 'monism'. The German Monist League he founded combined scientifically based ecological holism with *völkisch* social views. Haeckel believed in Nordic racial superiority, strenuously opposed race mixing and enthusiastically supported racial eugenics. His fervent nationalism became fanatical with the onset of World War I, and he fulminated in antisemitic tones against the post-war Council Republic in Bavaria.

In this way "Haeckel contributed to that special variety of German thought which served as the seed bed for National Socialism. He became one of Germany's major ideologists for racism, nationalism and imperialism."[10] Near the end of his life he joined the Thule Society, "a secret, radically right-wing organization which played a key role in the establishment of the Nazi movement."[11] But more than merely personal continuities are at stake here. The pioneer of scientific ecology, along with his disciples Willibald Hentschel, Wilhelm Bölsche and Bruno Wille, profoundly shaped the thinking of subsequent generations of environmentalists by embedding concern for the natural world in a tightly woven web of regressive social themes. From its very beginnings, then, ecology was bound up in an intensely reactionary political framework.

The specific contours of this early marriage of ecology and authoritarian social views are highly instructive. At the center of this ideological complex is the direct, unmediated application of biological categories to the social realm. Haeckel held that "civilization and the life of nations are governed by the same laws as prevail throughout nature and organic life."[12] This notion of 'natural laws' or 'natural order' has long been a mainstay of reactionary environmental thought. Its concomitant is anti-humanism:

> Thus, for the Monists, perhaps the most pernicious feature of European bourgeois civilization was the inflated importance which it attached to the idea of man in general, to his existence and to his talents, and to the belief that through his unique rational faculties man could essentially recreate the world and bring about a universally more harmonious and ethically just social order. [Humankind was] an insignificant creature when viewed as part of and measured against the vastness of the cosmos and the overwhelming forces of nature.[13]

Other Monists extended this anti-humanist emphasis and mixed it with the traditional *völkisch* motifs of indiscriminate anti-industrialism and anti-urbanism as well as the newly emerging pseudo-scientific racism. The linchpin, once again, was the conflation of biological and social categories. The biologist Raoul Francé, founding member of the Monist League, elaborated so-called *Lebensgesetze*, 'laws of life' through which the natural order determines the social order.

He opposed racial mixing, for example, as "unnatural." Francé is acclaimed by contemporary ecofascists as a "pioneer of the ecology movement."[14]

Francé's colleague Ludwig Woltmann, another student of Haeckel, insisted on a biological interpretation for all societal phenomena, from cultural attitudes to economic arrangements. He stressed the supposed connection between environmental purity and 'racial' purity: "Woltmann took a negative attitude toward modern industrialism. He claimed that the change from an agrarian to an industrial society had hastened the decline of the race. In contrast to nature, which engendered the harmonic forms of Germanism, there were the big cities, diabolical and inorganic, destroying the virtues of the race."[15]

Thus by the early years of the twentieth century a certain type of 'ecological' argumentation, saturated with right-wing political content, had attained a measure of respectability within the political culture of Germany. During the turbulent period surrounding World War I, the mixture of ethnocentric fanaticism, regressive rejection of modernity and genuine environmental concern proved to be a very potent potion indeed.

The Youth Movement and the Weimar Era

The chief vehicle for carrying this ideological constellation to prominence was the youth movement, an amorphous phenomenon which played a decisive but highly ambivalent role in shaping German popular culture during the first three tumultuous decades of this century. Also known as the *Wandervögel* (which translates roughly as 'wandering free spirits'), the youth movement was a hodge-podge of countercultural elements, blending neo-Romanticism, Eastern philosophies, nature mysticism, hostility to reason, and a strong communal impulse in a confused but no less ardent search for authentic, non-alienated social relations. Their back-to-the-land emphasis spurred a passionate sensitivity to the natural world and the damage it suffered. They have been aptly characterized as 'right-wing hippies,' for although some sectors of the movement gravitated toward various forms of emancipatory politics (though usually shedding their environmentalist trappings in the process), most of the *Wandervögel* were eventually absorbed by the Nazis. This shift from nature worship to *Führer* worship is worth examining.

The various strands of the youth movement shared a common self-conception: they were a purportedly 'non-political' response to a deep cultural crisis, stressing the primacy of direct emotional experience over social critique and action. They pushed the contradictions of their time to the breaking point, but were unable or unwilling to take the final step toward organized, focused social rebellion, "convinced that the changes they wanted to effect in society could not be brought about by political means, but only by the improvement of the individual."[16] This proved to be a fatal error. "Broadly speaking, two ways of revolt were open to them: they could have pursued their radical critique of society, which in due course would have brought them into the camp of social revolution. [But] the *Wandervögel* chose the other form of protest against society—romanticism."[17]

This posture lent itself all too readily to a very different kind of political mobilization: the 'unpolitical' zealotry of

21

fascism. The youth movement did not simply fail in its chosen form of protest, it was actively realigned when its members went over to the Nazis by the thousands. Its countercultural energies and its dreams of harmony with nature bore the bitterest fruit. This is, perhaps, the unavoidable trajectory of any movement which acknowledges and opposes social and ecological problems but does not recognize their systemic roots or actively resist the political and economic structures which generate them. Eschewing societal transformation in favor of personal change, an ostensibly apolitical disaffection can, in times of crisis, yield barbaric results.

The attraction such perspectives exercised on idealistic youth is clear: the enormity of the crisis seemed to enjoin a total rejection of its apparent causes. It is in the specific form of this rejection that the danger lies. Here the work of several more theoretical minds from the period is instructive. The philosopher Ludwig Klages profoundly influenced the youth movement and particularly shaped their ecological consciousness. He authored a tremendously important essay titled "Man and Earth" for the legendary Meissner gathering of the *Wandervögel* in 1913.[18] An extraordinarily poignant text and the best known of all Klages' work, it is not only "one of the very greatest manifestoes of the radical ecopacifist movement in Germany,"[19] but also a classic example of the seductive terminology of reactionary ecology.

"Man and Earth" anticipated just about all of the themes of the contemporary ecology movement. It decried the accelerating extinction of species, disturbance of global ecosystemic balance, deforestation, destruction of aboriginal peoples and of wild habitats, urban sprawl, and the increasing alienation of people from nature. In emphatic terms it disparaged Christianity, capitalism, economic utilitarianism, hyperconsumption and the ideology of 'progress.' It even condemned the environmental destructiveness of rampant tourism and the slaughter of whales, and displayed a clear recognition of the planet as an ecological totality. All of this in 1913!

It may come as a surprise, then, to learn that Klages was throughout his life politically archconservative and a venomous antisemite. One historian labels him a "Volkish fanatic" and another considers him simply "an intellectual pacemaker for the Third Reich" who "paved the way for fascist philosophy in many important respects."[20] In "Man and Earth" a genuine outrage at the devastation of the natural environment is coupled with a political subtext of cultural despair.[21] Klages' diagnosis of the ills of modern society, for all its declamations about capitalism, returns always to a single culprit: "Geist." His idiosyncratic use of this term, which means mind or intellect, was meant to denounce not only hyperrationalism or instrumental reason, but rational thought itself. Such a wholesale indictment of reason cannot help but have savage political implications. It forecloses any chance of rationally reconstructing society's relationship with nature and justifies the most brutal authoritarianism. But the lessons of Klages' life and work have been hard for ecologists to learn. In 1980, "Man and Earth" was republished as an esteemed and seminal treatise to accompany the birth of the German Greens.

Another philosopher and stern critic of Enlightenment who helped bridge fascism and environmentalism was Martin Heidegger. A much more renowned thinker than Klages, Heidegger preached "authentic Being" and harshly criticized modern technology, and is therefore often celebrated as a precursor of ecological thinking. On the basis of his critique of technology and rejection of humanism, contemporary deep ecologists have elevated Heidegger to their pantheon of eco-heroes:

> Heidegger's critique of anthropocentric humanism, his call for humanity to learn to "let things be," his notion that humanity is involved in a "play" or "dance" with earth, sky, and gods, his meditation on the possibility of an authentic mode of "dwelling" on the earth, his complaint that industrial technology is laying waste to the earth, his emphasis on the importance of local place and "homeland," his claim that humanity should guard and preserve things, instead of dominating them—all these aspects of Heidegger's thought help to support the claim that he is a major deep ecological theorist.[22]

Such effusions are, at best, dangerously naive. They suggest a style of thought utterly oblivious to the history of fascist appropriations of *all* the elements the quoted passage praises in Heidegger. (To his credit, the author of the above lines, a major deep ecological theorist in his own right, has since changed his position and eloquently urged his colleagues to do the same.)[23] As for the philosopher of Being himself, he was— unlike Klages, who lived in Switzerland after 1915—an active member of the Nazi party and for a time enthusiastically, even adoringly supported the *Führer*. His mystical panegyrics to *Heimat* (homeland) were complemented by a deep antisemitism, and his metaphysically phrased broadsides against technology and modernity converged neatly with populist demagogy. Although he lived and taught for thirty years after the fall of the Third Reich, Heidegger never once publicly regretted, much less renounced, his involvement with National Socialism, nor even perfunctorily condemned its crimes. His work, whatever its philosophical merits, stands today as a signal admonition about the political uses of anti-humanism in ecological garb.

In addition to the youth movement and proto-fascist philosophies, there were, of course, practical efforts at protecting natural habitats during the Weimar period. Many of these projects were profoundly implicated in the ideology which culminated in the victory of 'Blood and Soil.' A 1923 recruitment pitch for a woodlands preservation outfit gives a sense of the environmental rhetoric of the time:

> In every German breast the German forest quivers with its caverns and ravines, crags and boulders, waters and winds, legends and fairy tales, with its songs and its melodies, and awakens a powerful yearning and a longing for home; in all German souls the German forest lives and weaves with its depth and breadth, its stillness and strength, its might and dignity, its riches and its beauty—it is the source of German inwardness, of the German soul, of German freedom. Therefore protect and care for the German forest for the sake of the elders and the youth, and join the new German "League for the Protection and Consecration of the German Forest."[24]

The mantra-like repetition of the word "German" and the mystical depiction of the sacred forest fuse together, once again, nationalism and naturalism. This intertwinement took on a grisly significance with the collapse of the Weimar republic. For alongside such relatively innocuous conservation groups, another organization was growing which offered these ideas a hospitable home: the National Socialist German Workers Party, known by its acronym NSDAP. Drawing on the heritage of Arndt, Riehl, Haeckel, and others (all of whom were honored between 1933 and 1945 as forebears of triumphant National Socialism), the Nazi movement's incorporation of environmentalist themes was a crucial factor in its rise to popularity and state power.

Nature in National Socialist Ideology

The reactionary ecological ideas whose outlines are sketched above exerted a powerful and lasting influence on many of the central figures in the NSDAP. Weimar culture, after all, was fairly awash in such theories, but the Nazis gave them a peculiar inflection. The National Socialist "religion of nature," as one historian has described it, was a volatile admixture of primeval Teutonic nature mysticism, pseudo-scientific ecology, irrationalist anti-humanism, and a mythology of racial salvation through a return to the land. Its predominant themes were 'natural order,' organicist holism and denigration of humanity: "Throughout the writings, not only of Hitler, but of most Nazi ideologues, one can discern a fundamental deprecation of humans *vis-à-vis* nature, and, as a logical corollary to this, an attack upon human efforts to master nature."[25] Quoting a Nazi educator, the same source continues: "anthropocentric views in general had to be rejected. They would be valid only 'if it is assumed that nature has been created only for man. We decisively reject this attitude. According to our conception of nature, man is a link in the living chain of nature just as any other organism."[26]

Such arguments have a chilling currency within contemporary ecological discourse: the key to social-ecological harmony is ascertaining "the eternal laws of nature's processes" (Hitler) and organizing society to correspond to them. The *Führer* was particularly fond of stressing the "helplessness of humankind in the face of nature's everlasting law."[27] Echoing Haeckel and the Monists, *Mein Kampf* announces: "When people attempt to rebel against the iron logic of nature, they come into conflict with the very same principles to which they owe their existence as human beings. Their actions against nature must lead to their own downfall."[28]

The authoritarian implications of this view of humanity and nature become even clearer in the context of the Nazis' emphasis on holism and organicism. In 1934 the director of the Reich Agency for Nature Protection, Walter Schoenichen, established the following objectives for biology curricula: "Very early, the youth must develop an understanding of the civic importance of the 'organism', i.e. the co-ordination of all parts and organs for the benefit of the one and superior task of life."[29] This (by now familiar) unmediated adaptation of biological concepts to social phenomena served to justify not only the totalitarian social order of the Third Reich but also the expansionist politics of *Lebensraum* (the plan of conquering 'living space' in Eastern Europe for the German people). It also provided the link between environmental purity and racial purity:

> Two central themes of biology education follow [according to the Nazis] from the holistic perspective: nature protection and eugenics. If one views nature as a unified whole, students will automatically develop a sense for ecology and environmental conservation. At the same time, the nature protection concept will direct attention to the urbanized and 'overcivilized' modern human race.[30]

In many varieties of the National Socialist world view ecological themes were linked with traditional agrarian romanticism and hostility to urban civilization, all revolving around the idea of rootedness in nature. This conceptual constellation, especially the search for a lost connection to nature, was most pronounced among the neo-pagan elements in the Nazi leadership, above all Heinrich Himmler, Alfred Rosenberg, and Walther Darré. Rosenberg wrote in his colossal *The Myth of the 20th Century:* "Today we see the steady stream from the countryside to the city, deadly for the *Volk.* The cities swell ever larger, unnerving the *Volk* and destroying the threads which bind humanity to nature; they attract adventurers and profiteers of all colors, thereby fostering racial chaos."[31]

Such musings, it must be stressed, were not mere rhetoric; they reflected firmly held beliefs and, indeed, practices at the very top of the Nazi hierarchy which are today conventionally associated with ecological attitudes. Hitler and Himmler were both strict vegetarians and animal lovers, attracted to nature mysticism and homeopathic cures, and staunchly opposed to vivisection and cruelty to animals. Himmler even established experimental organic farms to grow herbs for SS medicinal purposes. And Hitler, at times, could sound like a veritable Green utopian, discussing authoritatively and in detail various renewable energy sources (including environmentally appropriate hydropower and producing natural gas from sludge) as alternatives to coal, and declaring "water, winds and tides" the energy path of the future.[32]

Even in the midst of war, Nazi leaders maintained their commitment to ecological ideals which were, for them, an essential element of racial rejuvenation. In December 1942, Himmler released a decree "On the Treatment of the Land in the Eastern Territories," referring to the newly annexed portions of Poland. It read in part:

> The peasant of our racial stock has always carefully endeavored to increase the natural powers of the soil, plants, and animals, and to preserve the balance of the whole of nature. For him, respect for divine creation is the measure of all culture. If, therefore, the new *Lebensräume* (living spaces) are to become a homeland for our settlers, the planned arrangement of the landscape to keep it close to nature is a decisive prerequisite. It is one of the bases for fortifying the German *Volk*.[33]

This passage recapitulates almost all of the tropes comprised by classical ecofascist ideology: *Lebensraum, Heimat,* the agrarian mystique, the health of the *Volk,* closeness to and respect for nature (explicitly constructed as the standard against which society is to be judged), maintaining nature's precarious balance, and the earthy powers of the soil and its creatures. Such motifs were anything but personal idiosyncrasies on the part of Hitler, Himmler, or Rosenberg;

even Göring—who was, along with Goebbels, the member of the Nazi inner circle least hospitable to ecological ideas—appeared at times to be a committed conservationist.[34] These sympathies were also hardly restricted to the upper echelons of the party. A study of the membership rolls of several mainstream Weimar era *Naturschutz* (nature protection) organizations revealed that by 1939, fully 60 percent of these conservationists had joined the NSDAP (compared to about 10 percent of adult men and 25 percent of teachers and lawyers).[35] Clearly the affinities between environmentalism and National Socialism ran deep.

At the level of ideology, then, ecological themes played a vital role in German fascism. It would be a grave mistake, however, to treat these elements as mere propaganda, cleverly deployed to mask Nazism's true character as a technocratic-industrialist juggernaut. The definitive history of German anti-urbanism and agrarian romanticism argues incisively against this view:

> Nothing could be more wrong than to suppose that most of the leading National Socialist ideologues had cynically feigned an agrarian romanticism and hostility to urban culture, without any inner conviction and for merely electoral and propaganda purposes, in order to hoodwink the public … In reality, the majority of the leading National Socialist ideologists were without any doubt more or less inclined to agrarian romanticism and anti-urbanism and convinced of the need for a relative re-agrarianization.[36]

The question remains, however: To what extent did the Nazis actually implement environmental policies during the twelve-year Reich? There is strong evidence that the 'ecological' tendency in the party, though largely ignored today, had considerable success for most of the party's reign. This "green wing" of the NSDAP was represented above all by Walther Darré, Fritz Todt, Alwin Seifert and Rudolf Hess, the four figures who primarily shaped fascist ecology in practice.

Blood and Soil as Official Doctrine

"The unity of blood and soil must be restored," proclaimed Richard Walther Darré in 1930.[37] This infamous phrase denoted a quasi-mystical connection between 'blood' (the race or *Volk*) and 'soil' (the land and the natural environment) specific to Germanic peoples and absent, for example, among Celts and Slavs. For the enthusiasts of *Blut und Boden*, the Jews especially were a rootless, wandering people, incapable of any true relationship with the land. German blood, in other words, engendered an exclusive claim to the sacred German soil. While the term "blood and soil" had been circulating in *völkisch* circles since at least the Wilhelmine era, it was Darré who first popularized it as a slogan and then enshrined it as a guiding principle of Nazi thought. Harking back to Arndt and Riehl, he envisioned a thoroughgoing ruralization of Germany and Europe, predicated on a revitalized yeoman peasantry, in order to ensure racial health and ecological sustainability.

Darré was one of the party's chief "race theorists" and was also instrumental in galvanizing peasant support for the Nazis during the critical period of the early 1930s. From 1933 until 1942 he held the posts of Reich Peasant Leader and Minister of Agriculture. This was no minor fiefdom; the agriculture

31

ministry had the fourth largest budget of all the myriad Nazi ministries even well into the war.[38] From this position Darré was able to lend vital support to various ecologically oriented initiatives. He played an essential part in unifying the nebulous proto-environmentalist tendencies in National Socialism:

> It was Darré who gave the ill-defined anti-civilization, anti-liberal, anti-modern and latent anti-urban sentiments of the Nazi elite a foundation in the agrarian mystique. And it seems as if Darré had an immense influence on the ideology of National Socialism, as if he was able to articulate significantly more clearly than before the value system of an agrarian society contained in Nazi ideology and—above all—to legitimate this agrarian model and give Nazi policy a goal that was clearly oriented toward a far-reaching re-agrarianization.[39]

This goal was not only quite consonant with imperialist expansion in the name of *Lebensraum*, it was in fact one of its primary justifications, even motivations. In language replete with the biologistic metaphors of organicism, Darré declared: "The concept of Blood and Soil gives us the moral right to take back as much land in the East as is necessary to establish a harmony between the body of our *Volk* and the geopolitical space."[40]

Aside from providing green camouflage for the colonization of Eastern Europe, Darré worked to install environmentally sensitive principles as the very basis of the Third Reich's agricultural policy. Even in its most productivist phases, these precepts remained emblematic of Nazi doctrine. When the "Battle for Production" (a scheme to boost the productivity of the agricultural sector) was proclaimed at the second Reich Farmers Congress in 1934, the very first point in the program read "Keep the soil healthy!" But Darré's most important innovation was the introduction on a large scale of organic farming methods, significantly labeled "lebensgesetzliche Landbauweise," or farming according to the laws of life. The term points up yet again the natural order ideology which underlies so much reactionary ecological thought. The impetus for these unprecedented measures came from Rudolf Steiner's anthroposophy and its techniques of biodynamic cultivation.[41]

The campaign to institutionalize organic farming encompassed tens of thousands of smallholdings and estates across Germany. It met with considerable resistance from other members of the Nazi hierarchy, above all Backe and Göring. But Darré, with the help of Hess and others, was able to sustain the policy until his forced resignation in 1942 (an event which had little to do with his environmentalist leanings). And these efforts in no sense represented merely Darré's personal predilections; as the standard history of German agricultural policy points out, Hitler and Himmler "were in complete sympathy with these ideas."[42] Still, it was largely Darré's influence in the Nazi apparatus which yielded, in practice, a level of government support for ecologically sound farming methods and land use planning unmatched by any state before or since.

For these reasons Darré has sometimes been regarded as a forerunner of the contemporary Green movement. His biographer, in fact, once referred to him as the "father of the Greens."[43] Her book *Blood and Soil*, undoubtedly the best single source on Darré in either German or English, consistently downplays the virulently fascist elements in his thinking, portraying him instead as a misguided agrarian radical. This grave error in judgement indicates the powerfully disorienting pull of an 'ecological' aura. Darré's published writings alone, dating back to the early twenties, are enough to indict him as a rabidly racist and jingoist ideologue particularly prone to a vulgar and hateful antisemitism (he spoke of Jews, revealingly, as "weeds"). His decade-long tenure as a loyal servant and, moreover, architect of the Nazi state demonstrates his dedication to Hitler's deranged cause. One account even claims that it was Darré who convinced Hitler and Himmler of the necessity of exterminating the Jews and Slavs.[44] The ecological aspects of his thought cannot, in sum, be separated from their thoroughly Nazi framework. Far from embodying the 'redeeming' facets of National Socialism, Darré represents the baleful specter of ecofascism in power.

Implementing the Ecofascist Program

It is frequently pointed out that the agrarian and romantic moments in Nazi ideology and policy were in constant tension with, if not in flat contradiction to, the technocratic-industrialist thrust of the Third Reich's rapid modernization. What is not often remarked is that even these modernizing tendencies had a significant ecological component. The two men principally responsible for sustaining this environmentalist commitment in the midst of intensive industrialization were *Reichsminister* Fritz Todt and his aide, the high-level planner and engineer Alwin Seifert.

Todt was "one of the most influential National Socialists,"[45] directly responsible for questions of technological and industrial policy. At his death in 1942 he headed three different cabinet-level ministries in addition to the enormous quasi-official *Organisation Todt*, and had "gathered the major technical tasks of the Reich into his own hands."[46] According to his successor, Albert Speer, Todt "loved nature" and "repeatedly had serious run-ins with Bormann, protesting against his despoiling the landscape around Obersalzberg."[47] Another source calls him simply "an ecologist."[48] This reputation is based chiefly on Todt's efforts to make Autobahn construction—one of the largest building enterprises undertaken in this century—as environmentally sensitive as possible.

The pre-eminent historian of German engineering describes this commitment thus: "Todt demanded of the completed work of technology a harmony with nature and with the landscape, thereby fulfilling modern ecological principles of engineering as well as the 'organological' principles of his own era along with their roots in *völkisch* ideology."[49] The ecological aspects of this approach to construction went well beyond an emphasis on harmonious adaptation to the natural surroundings for aesthetic reasons; Todt also established strict criteria for respecting wetlands, forests and ecologically sensitive areas. But just as with Arndt, Riehl and Darré, these environmentalist concerns were inseparably bound to a *völkisch*-nationalist outlook. Todt himself expressed this connection succinctly: "The fulfillment of mere transportation purposes is not the final aim of German highway construction. The German highway must be an expression of its surrounding landscape and an expression of the German essence."[50]

Todt's chief advisor and collaborator on environmental issues was his lieutenant Alwin Seifert, whom Todt reportedly once called a "fanatical ecologist."[51] Seifert bore the official title of Reich Advocate for the Landscape, but his nickname within the party was "Mr. Mother Earth." The appellation was deserved; Seifert dreamed of a "total conversion from technology to nature,"[52] and would often wax lyrical about the wonders of German nature and the tragedy of "humankind's" carelessness. As early as 1934 he wrote to Hess demanding attention to water issues and invoking "work methods that are more attuned to nature."[53] In discharging his official duties Seifert stressed the importance of wilderness and energetically opposed monoculture, wetlands drainage and chemicalized agriculture. He criticized Darré as too moderate, and "called for an agricultural revolution towards 'a more peasant-like, natural, simple' method of farming, 'independent of capital.'"[54]

With the Third Reich's technological policy entrusted to figures such as these, even the Nazis' massive industrial build-up took on a distinctively green hue. The prominence of nature in the party's philosophical background helped ensure that more radical initiatives often received a sympathetic hearing in the highest offices of the Nazi state. In the mid-thirties Todt and Seifert vigorously pushed for an all-encompassing Reich Law for the Protection of Mother Earth "in order to stem the steady loss of this irreplaceable basis of all life."[55] Seifert reports that all of the ministries were prepared to co-operate save one; only the minister of the economy opposed the bill because of its impact on mining.

But even near-misses such as these would have been unthinkable without the support of Reich Minister Rudolf Hess, who provided the "green wing" of the NSDAP a secure anchor at the very top of the party hierarchy. It would be difficult to overestimate Hess's power and centrality in the complex governmental machinery of the National Socialist regime. He joined the party in 1920 as member #16, and for two decades was Hitler's devoted personal deputy. He has been described as "Hitler's closest confidant,"[56] and the *Führer* himself referred to Hess as his "closest advisor."[57] Hess was not only the highest party leader and second in line (after Göring) to succeed Hitler; in addition, all legislation and every decree had to pass through his office before becoming law.

An inveterate nature lover as well as a devout Steinerite, Hess insisted on a strictly biodynamic diet—not even Hitler's rigorous vegetarian standards were good enough for him—and accepted only homeopathic medicines. It was Hess who introduced Darré to Hitler, thus securing the "green wing" its first power base. He was an even more tenacious proponent of organic farming than Darré, and pushed the latter to take more demonstrative steps in support of the *lebensgesetzliche Landbauweise*.[58] His office was also directly responsible for land use planning across the Reich, employing a number of specialists who shared Seifert's ecological approach.[59]

With Hess's enthusiastic backing, the "green wing" was able to achieve its most notable successes. As early as March 1933, a wide array of environmentalist legislation was approved and implemented at national, regional and local levels. These measures, which included reforestation programs, bills protecting animal and plant species, and preservationist decrees blocking industrial development, undoubtedly "ranked among the most progressive in the world at that time."[60] Planning ordinances were designed for the protection of wildlife habitat and at the same time demanded respect for the sacred German forest. The Nazi state also created the first nature preserves in Europe.

Along with Darré's efforts toward re-agrarianization and support for organic agriculture, as well as Todt and Seifert's attempts to institutionalize an environmentally sensitive land use planning and industrial policy, the major accomplishment of the Nazi ecologists was the *Reichsnaturschutzgesetz* of 1935. This completely unprecedented "nature protection law" not only established guidelines for safeguarding flora, fauna, and "natural monuments" across the Reich; it also restricted commercial access to remaining tracts of wilderness. In addition, the comprehensive ordinance "required all national, state and local officials to consult with Naturschutz authorities in a timely manner before undertaking any measures that would produce fundamental alterations in the countryside."[61]

Although the legislation's effectiveness was questionable, traditional German environmentalists were overjoyed at its passage. Walter Schoenichen declared it the "definitive fulfillment of the *völkisch*-romantic longings,"[62] and Hans Klose, Schoenichen's successor as head of the Reich Agency for Nature Protection, described Nazi environmental policy as the "high point of nature protection" in Germany. Perhaps the greatest success of these measures was in facilitating the "intellectual realignment of German Naturschutz" and the integration of mainstream environmentalism into the Nazi enterprise.[63]

While the achievements of the "green wing" were daunting, they should not be exaggerated. Ecological initiatives were, of course, hardly universally popular within the party. Goebbels, Bormann, and Heydrich, for example, were implacably opposed to them, and considered Darré, Hess and their fellows undependable dreamers, eccentrics, or simply security risks. This latter suspicion seemed to be confirmed by Hess's famed flight to Britain in 1941; after that point, the environmentalist tendency was for the most part suppressed. Todt was killed in a plane crash in February 1942, and shortly thereafter Darré was stripped of all his posts. For the final three years of the Nazi conflagration the "green wing" played no active role. Their work, however, had long since left an indelible stain.

Fascist Ecology in Context

To make this dismaying and discomforting analysis more palatable, it is tempting to draw precisely the wrong conclusion—namely, that even the most reprehensible political undertakings sometimes produce laudable results. But the real lesson here is just the opposite: Even the most laudable of causes can be perverted and instrumentalized in the service of criminal savagery. The "green wing" of the NSDAP was not a group of innocents, confused and manipulated idealists, or reformers from within; they were conscious promoters and executors of a vile program explicitly dedicated to inhuman racist violence, massive political repression and worldwide military domination. Their 'ecological' involvements, far from offsetting these fundamental commitments, deepened

39

and radicalized them. In the end, their configuration of environmental politics was directly and substantially responsible for organized mass murder.

No aspect of the Nazi project can be properly understood without examining its implication in the holocaust. Here, too, ecological arguments played a crucially malevolent role. Not only did the "green wing" refurbish the sanguine antisemitism of traditional reactionary ecology; it catalyzed a whole new outburst of lurid racist fantasies of organic inviolability and political revenge. The confluence of anti-humanist dogma with a fetishization of natural 'purity' provided not merely a rationale but an incentive for the Third Reich's most heinous crimes. Its insidious appeal unleashed murderous energies previously untapped. Finally, the displacement of any social analysis of environmental destruction in favor of mystical ecology served as an integral component in the preparation of the final solution:

> To explain the destruction of the countryside and environmental damage, without questioning the German people's bond to nature, could only be done by not analysing environmental damage in a societal context and by refusing to understand them as an expression of conflicting social interests. Had this been done, it would have led to criticism of National Socialism itself since that was not immune to such forces. One solution was to associate such environmental problems with the destructive influence of other races. National Socialism could then be seen to strive for the elimination of other races in order to allow the German people's innate understanding and feeling of nature to assert itself, hence securing a harmonic life close to nature for the future.[64]

This is the true legacy of ecofascism in power: "genocide developed into a necessity under the cloak of environment protection."[65]

The experience of the "green wing" of German fascism is a sobering reminder of the political volatility of ecology. It certainly does not indicate any inherent or inevitable connection between ecological issues and right-wing politics; alongside the reactionary tradition surveyed here, there has always been an equally vital heritage of left-libertarian ecology, in Germany as elsewhere.[66] But certain patterns can be discerned: "While concerns about problems posed by humankind's increasing mastery over nature have increasingly been shared by ever larger groups of people embracing a plethora of ideologies, the most consistent 'pro-natural order' response found political embodiment on the radical right."[67] This is the common thread which unites merely conservative or even supposedly apolitical manifestations of environmentalism with the straightforwardly fascist variety.

The historical record does, to be sure, belie the vacuous claim that "those who want to reform society according to nature are neither left nor right but ecologically minded."[68] Environmental themes can be mobilized from the left or from the right, indeed they *require* an explicit social context if they are to have any political valence whatsoever. "Ecology" alone does not prescribe a politics; it must be interpreted, mediated through some theory of society in order to acquire political meaning. Failure to heed this mediated interrelationship between the social and the ecological is the hallmark of reactionary ecology.

As noted above, this failure most commonly takes the form of a call to "reform society according to nature," that is, to formulate some version of 'natural order' or 'natural law' and submit human needs and actions to it. As a consequence, the underlying social processes and societal structures which constitute and shape people's relations with their environment are left unexamined. Such willful ignorance, in turn, obscures the ways in which all conceptions of nature are themselves socially produced, and leaves power structures unquestioned while simultaneously providing them with apparently 'naturally ordained' status. Thus the substitution of eco-mysticism for clear-sighted social-ecological inquiry has catastrophic political repercussions, as the complexity of the society-nature dialectic is collapsed into a purified Oneness. An ideologically charged 'natural order' does not leave room for compromise; its claims are absolute.

For all of these reasons, the slogan advanced by many contemporary Greens, "We are neither right nor left but up front," is historically naive and politically fatal. The necessary project of creating an emancipatory ecological politics demands an acute awareness and understanding of the legacy of classical ecofascism and its conceptual continuities with present-day environmental discourse. An 'ecological' orientation alone, outside of a critical social framework, is dangerously unstable. The record of fascist ecology shows that under the right conditions such an orientation can quickly lead to barbarism.

JANET BIEHL

"ECOLOGY" AND THE MODERNIZATION OF FASCISM IN THE GERMAN ULTRA-RIGHT

It is an incontestable fact that the ecology crisis today is real. In a vast number of ways and places, the biosphere of this planet is undergoing a great deal of damage. Parts of the environment have already been rendered uninhabitable through toxic wastes and nuclear power plant disasters, while systemic pollution, ozone holes, global warming, and other disasters are increasingly tearing the fabric on which all life depends. That such damage is wrought overwhelmingly by corporations in a competitive international market economy has never been clearer, while the need to replace the existing society with one such as social ecology advances has never been more urgent.[1]

At a time when worsening economic conditions and strong political disaffection occur along with ecological dislocations, however, nationalist and even fascist ideas are gaining an increasingly high profile in Europe, particularly, but not only, in the Federal Republic of Germany. With social tensions exacerbated, neofascist groups of various kinds are winning electoral representation, even as their loosely linked cohorts commit acts of violence against foreigners. Such groups, both skinhead and "intellectual," are part of a "New" Right that explicitly draws its ideas from classical fascism. They are updating the old nationalist, mystical, and misanthropic themes of the "Old" Right, writes Jutta Ditfurth, in a "modernization of fascism." Among other things, they are using a right-wing interpretation of ecology "as an ideological 'hinge' for organizing the extreme-right and neofascist scene."[2]

Today's fascists have a distinct ideological legacy from their fascist forebears upon which to draw. Indeed, "ecology" and a mystical reverence for the natural world are hardly new to German nationalism. At the end of the nineteenth century, a cultural revolt against positivism swept much of Europe, as George L. Mosse writes, and in Germany it became infused with both nature-mysticism and racial nationalism. This revolt

> became intimately bound up with a belief in nature's cosmic life force, a dark force whose mysteries could be understood, not through science, but through the occult. An ideology based upon such premises was fused with the glories of an Aryan past, and in turn, that past received a thoroughly romantic and mystical interpretation.[3]

Culminating in the 1920s, an assortment of occult and pseudo-scientific ideas coalesced around the idea of a German *Volk* into a romantic nationalism, romantic racism, and a mystical nature-worshipping faith. Indeed, as Mosse observes, the German word

> *Volk* is a much more comprehensive term than "people," for to German thinkers ever since the birth of German romanticism in the late eighteenth century "Volk" signified the union of a group of people with a transcendental "essence." This "essence" might be called "nature" or "cosmos" or "mythos," but in each instance it was fused to man's innermost nature, and represented the source of his creativity, his depth of feeling, his individuality, and his unity with other members of the Volk.[4]

The *völkisch* movement of the 1920s regarded modern materialism, urbanism, rationalism, and science as artificial and evil, alien to this "essence."[5] In a time of bitter social dislocation, it saw Weimar democracy as the product of Western democratic and liberal ideals and, further, as a puppet regime controlled by people who did not represent German "essence." Many alleged that a Jewish world conspiracy lay behind the discontents of modernism, including materialistic consumerism, soulless industrialism, a homogenized commercial culture, and excessive modern technology, all of which were said to be systematically destroying traditional German values. Only true patriots could save Germans from ruin, thought the extreme right—themselves.

This movement sought to assert a truly Germanic alternative—one as racialist as it was nationalist in nature. The popular writings of Paul Lagarde and Julius Langbehn favored an aristocratic social order in which Germans would rule the world. It invoked a nature-romanticism in which a closeness to the natural landscape was to give people a heightened sense of aliveness and "authenticity." It advanced a new cosmic faith, embodied in "Aryan" blood, that was to be grasped through intuition rather than science in a plethora of occult and esoteric spiritualistic faiths that abounded in Germany in the 1920s. Mystical belief-systems like Theosophy, Anthroposophy, and Ariosophy (a mystical Aryanism) abounded and were rife with Germanic nationalist components, such that they could be used to mystify an "ecological" nationalism.

However inadvertently, the romantic nationalists of the *völkisch* movement became an important source for National Socialist ideology, which ironically drew on its antimodern sentiments even as it built a technologically modern and virulently nationalistic and genocidal totalitarian state. Demagogically appealing to a very real sense of alienation, the Nazis stage-managed indoctrination extravaganzas that promised "authenticity" in a mystical, romantic nationalism that was "closer to nature," even as they engaged in mass murder. Stressing the need to return to simpler, healthier, and more "natural" lifeways, they advanced the idea and practice of a "Nordic peasantry" tied organically to the soil—even as they constructed a society that was industrially more modernized and rationalized than any German society had seen to that time.

The so-called "New" Right today appeals to themes reminiscent of the *völkisch* movement in pre-Nazi Germany. It, too, presents itself as offering an "ecological" alternative to modern society. In the view of the "New" Right today, the destruction of the environment and the repression of nationalities have a common root in 'Semitic" monotheism and universalism. In its later form, Christianity, and in its subsequent secularized forms, liberalism and Marxism, this dualistic, homogenizing universalism is alleged to have brought on both the ecological crisis and the suppression of national identity. Just as Judeo-Christian universalism was destructive of authentic cultures when Christian missionaries went out into the world, so too is modernity eliminating ethnic and national cultures. Moreover, through the unbridled technology to which it gave rise, this modern universalism is said to have perpetrated not only the destruction of nature but an annihilation of the spirit; the destruction of nature, it is said, is life-threatening in the spiritual sense as well as the physical, since when people deny pristine nature, their access to their "authentic" self is blocked.

The dualistic yet universalistic "Semitic" legacy is borne today most egregiously, in "New" Right ideology, by the United States, in whose "mongrel" culture—egalitarian democracy— all cultures and races are mixed together, forming a crass, soulless society. American cultural imperialism is genocidal of other cultures around the world, and its technological imperialism is destroying the global environment. The fascist quest for "national identity" and ecological salvation seeks to counter "Western civilization"—that is, the United States, as opposed to "European civilization"—by advancing a notion of "ethnopluralism" that seeks for all cultures to have sovereignty over themselves and their environment. Europe should become, instead of a modernized monoculture, a "Europe of fatherlands," with autonomy for all its peoples.

Just as Turks should live in Turkey and Senegalese in Senegal, Germans should have Germany for themselves, "New" Right ideologues argue.

Ecology can easily be perverted to justify this "ethnopluralism"—that is, nationalism. Conceptions of one's region as one's "homeland," or *Heimat*, can be perverted into a nationalistic regionalism when a region's traditions and language are mystically tied to an "ancestral" landscape. (The word *Heimat* connotes as well a turn toward the past, an anti-urban mood, a familiar community, and proximity to nature. For several decades the concept was looked upon with disfavor because the Nazis had used it, but intellectuals rediscovered it in the 1970s, after further decades of capitalist industrialization.) For a people seeking to assert themselves against an outside intruder, an "ecologized" *Heimat* in which they are biologically embedded can become a useful tool not only against imperialism but against immigration, foreigners, and "overpopulation." Elaborate justifications for opposing Third World immigration are disguised as diversity, drawing on "ecological" arguments against "overpopulation." Today it is not only fascists who invoke *Heimat*; in September 1989, for example, the head of the respectable League for the Protection of the Environment and Nature (Bund für Umwelt- und Naturschutz, or BUND), environmentalist Hubert Weinzierl, remarked that

> only when humanity's main concern, the diminution of the stream of overpopulation, has been accomplished, will there be any meaning or any prospect of building an environment that is capable of improvement, of configuring the landscape of

our civilization in such a way that it remains worthy of being called *Heimat*.[6]

An ecology that is mystical, in turn, may become a justification for a nationalism that is mystical. In the New Age milieu of today, with its affinities for ecology, the ultra-right may well find the mystical component it needs to make a truly updated, modernized authoritarian nationalism. As in Germany between the two world wars, antirational cults of the New Age—primitivistic, esoteric—abound in both the Federal Republic and the Anglo-American world. Such antirationalism and mysticism are appealed to by the "New" Right; as anarchist publisher Wolfgang Haug observes, "The New Right, in effect, wants above all to redefine social norms so that rational doubt is regarded as decadent and eliminated, and new 'natural' norms are established." [7]

Neofascist "Ecology"

Ecology is warped for mystical-nationalist ends by a whole series of neofascist groups and parties. Indeed, so multifarious are the ecofascist parties that have arisen, and so much do their memberships overlap, that they form what antifascist researcher Volkmar Wölk calls an "ecofascist network."[8] Their programmatic literature often combines ecology and nationalism in ways that are designed to appeal to people who do not consider themselves fascists, while at the same time they ideologically support neo-Nazi street-fighting skinheads who commit acts of violence against foreigners.

National Revolutionaries[9]

The National Revolutionaries (NRs) manipulatively mix themes of left and right in their uses of nationalism and ecology, in an attempt to cross ideological lines. They draw on an old tenet of right-wing dissent in Germany—the belief that a "Third Way" between capitalism and socialism is necessary and that Germany is predestined to lead humankind toward it.[10] The NRs' "Third Way" is based on nationalism, a socialism "of the specific national way"[11]—in short, a "national socialism." A wing of the NRs today, called the Solidaristen, identifies itself with the Strasser brothers, two 1920s Nazi Party members who took the "socialism" in "National Socialism" seriously and represented the "left" anticapitalist wing of the Nazis. Today, the Solidaristen and other NRs regard Otto Strasser in particular as the "Trotsky of National Socialism" because of his 1920s intraparty power struggle with Hitler; Hitler's ejection of this fascist in 1930 was, for them, a betrayal of National Socialism.

Today's leading NR ideologist, Henning Eichberg, calls for the assertion of "national identity" and a "liberation nationalism." Seeking to appeal to left and right, NR publications have supported national liberation movements from across the traditional political spectrum, including the Irish, Basques, Ukrainians, and Afghans, as well as Sandinistas.[12] They regarded divided Germany as an occupied country, "the result of the imperialist politics of the occupation forces," and they sought to "liberate" it—including Austria. Now that Germany has been freed from this "occupation," the National Revolutionaries are free to concentrate on "reunifying" with Austria.

Eichberg regards Judeo-Christianity as the ultimate root of all present evils, since it is overly intellectual and alienates humanity both from itself and from the divine; it neglects the emotions and the body. Tied in as it is with the logic of productivism, Christianity, Eichberg writes, is the "religion of growth" that must be fought at all costs. To help cultivate "national identity," he proposes instead a new religion that mixes together neopagan Germanic, Celtic, and Indian religions with old *völkisch*-nationalistic ideas. It is to be based on "the sensuality-physicality of dance and ritual, ceremony and taboo, meditation, prayer, and ecstasy. In essence, [this religion] constitutes itself as a form of praxis" against the "religion of growth" since its "sensuous counter-experiences" can restore humanity to closer contact with nature. Sounding like many New Agers in the United States, Eichberg calls for a return to pristine nature, to the alleged primordial sources of people's lives, psyches, and authentic cultures, and for people to heal themselves within as part of healing the ecological crisis, overcoming their own alienation, and rediscovering themselves.[13]

National Revolutionaries exploit ecological themes not only to construct primitivistic New Age religions but for political activity as well. During the 1970s they organized around opposition to nuclear energy at about the same time as the citizens' initiative movement did. "With their ecological and antinuclear enthusiasm," observes Walter Laqueur,

> their cultural anti-Americanism and their support for movements of national liberation in many parts of the world,

the "national revolutionaries" tried, in fact, to outflank their left-wing contemporaries. Some regarded Sinn Fein as a model for the German national revolutionaries, others suggested "political Balkanization" in Germany and Europe as a solution to all outstanding questions.[14]

Other National Revolutionaries took a different political approach: at the end of the 1970s, they joined the newly emerging Greens, where some of their number succeeded in holding office for a time. In October 1980, the Alternative List of West Berlin, for one, decided they could not work with National Revolutionaries, whom they considered even more dangerous than overt neo-Nazis because they hid their true intentions behind a veil of grassroots democratic and ecological programs. They were mostly driven out of the Greens, at least as far as observers seem aware today.[15]

The Freedom German Workers Party[16]

Like the National Revolutionaries, the Freedom German Workers Party (Freiheitliche Deutsche Arbeiterpartei, or FAP) calls for a "national socialism," albeit one based on "a sense of community instead of class struggle." The FAP seeks no rapprochement with leftists; it openly and militantly proclaims its support for Nazi ideas, celebrates race and nation, and is pro-Hitler rather than Strasserite. It praises German soldiers, whose "achievements" in two world wars will "still be admired in a thousand years." The FAP is largely controlled by The Movement (Die Bewegung), which seeks to reestablish the NSDAP (the Nazi Party) in the Federal Republic and unite all fascist groups under its aegis.[17]

The FAP recruits from among skinheads and soccer fans, and its activities include acts of violence, arson, and racial attacks on foreigners. It advances the crudest "Germany for Germans—foreigners out" slogans.[18] When it engages in electoral activity, its programmatic demands have included "German jobs for German workers," "repatriation for foreigners," "no franchise for foreigners," and an end to the "crazy enthusiasm for integration."[19] Germans today must not ruin the "legacy of our fathers," the "cultural landscape"; Alsace-Lorraine, the South Tyrol, and Austria should all be returned to Germany.

FAP Nazis especially loathe "humanistically oriented cosmopolitanism." Marxism, liberalism, and Christianity "have torn humanity from its connectedness to the natural cycles of our earth." No "technical environmentalism" will succeed against the "increasingly obvious ecological catastrophe," they believe. Rather, the "disrupted relations between humanity and the rest of nature" require an "ecological revolution" and a "radical revolution in consciousness" that will "lead humanity to a reintegration with the structure of planetary life." We need a new ethics, they maintain, one in which "humanity, animals and nature are regarded as a unity. Animals are not things" but are "life-forms that feel joy and pain and need our protection." Not surprisingly, the FAP regards abortion as a "crime against the laws of a healthy nature and against God."

In a blatant self-contradiction, their concrete environmental demands are in fact friendly to capitalism: They want "continued economic growth," yet less profit-seeking. "Ecological necessities … must be brought into accordance with a functioning economy," they believe, while "the cyclical system of nature should ... be incorporated into the economic realm."

The Republicans[20]

The Republicans, a political party founded by former Waffen-SS member Franz Schönhuber in 1983, have made numerous disavowals of any association with the Nazis—they present themselves as nothing more than a "community of German patriots." Yet this does not stop them from taking explicitly anti-immigrant stances, especially against Turks, or from exploiting discontents about the influx of foreigners generally, or from maintaining that Germany should be "for Germans." The presence of a "tidal wave" of asylum-seekers in the Federal Republic, they believe, causes "the importation of criminals," "social tensions," and "financial burdens."

The Republicans call for the "preservation of the existence of the German *Volk*, its health and its ecological living-space [*Lebensraum*] as a priority for domestic policy. This goal," they add, "will also foster environmental protection." Indeed, ecological dislocations are endangering Germans" "health"— and by "health" they mean the "genetic health" of the German people. Such "health" has "a higher value than short-term profits and striving for a standard of living." Protecting and maintaining a "healthy environment" not only assures the "security of the means of life of our people" but is "a patriotic duty." The Republicans are stringently antiabortion for German women, yet for the Third World, "meaningful family planning" is necessary to end the "population explosion" and its consequent threat to the environment; without it there will be "natural catastrophe and starvation."

The National Democratic Party[21]

The National Democratic Party of Germany (Nationaldemokratische Partei Deutschlands, or NPD), founded in 1964 mainly by people who had been active Nazis before 1945, rose to prominence during the 1960s. This aggressively nationalist party long called for German reunification, while its programmatic literature complains that "two wars within one generation ... have eaten away at the substantive health of the German people." (It does not mention what those wars did to the Jews, as Ditfurth dryly notes.) The NPD laments the destruction of the environment, which "has disadvantageous effects on the *Volk*-health." Germans should not be exposed to "chemical dyes" and should be protected from "congenital illness," while people with AIDS should be required to "register." The "preservation" of the "German people" requires that German women prolifically give birth, and therefore the NPD is against the "devaluation and destruction of the family." Since abortion threatens "the biological existence of our people," women who have abortions should be punished. The party calls for maternal and housekeeping training for "feminine youth."

In 1973, the NPD drew up an "Ecological Manifesto" that invoked "the laws of nature" to justify a hierarchically structured, "organic" order that would govern social relationships.[22] It inveighs against "the environment polluted and poisoned by a humanity that lives increasingly isolated in a degraded mass," which "is only the most noticeable symptom of the ruined equilibrium of humanity and nature." In the years since then, the NPD's rhetoric has become increasingly New Age oriented; it now calls for "reachieving … an environmental consciousness, so necessary for life." Achieving this consciousness, the 1988 NPD program states, "first requires an inner revolution in human thought. It is not the unlimited accumulation of material goods or boundless consumption that gives meaning to human life and happiness, but the experience of nature, concern for cultural values, and social security in the family and *Volk*." Indeed, "*Volk*-consciousness and environmental consciousness are inseparable," since "millions of strangers" threaten "our *Volk* in its existence."

The German People's Union[23]

The German People's Union (Deutsche Volksunion, or DVU) was founded by Dr. Gerhard Frey (born in 1933), a longtime ultra-right activist and publisher. Still its leading figure, Frey has been fixated for decades on the Second World War in DVU publications, casting doubts on the concentration camps as they are normally depicted and generally denying German guilt; his publications offer Nazi memorabilia for sale. The DVU proclaims that "Germany should remain German" and calls for "priority in German housing for Germans" and "national identity and self-determination." For the DVU, environmental protection means passing "stringent laws against polluters," "strict examination of imported foodstuffs," and imposing restrictions on animal experimentation and on "the torture of animals." Protecting life means "an end to abortion abuse."

Anthroposophy and the World League
for the Protection of Life

Political parties like these have an assortment of "Old" Right—
that is, Nazi—connections upon which they may draw in their
search for "ecological" modernization. One such connection is
the World League for the Protection of Life (Weltbund Schutz
des Lebens, or WSL). This group is not without a certain general
appeal in the Federal Republic, since its outlook is based on
Anthroposophy, a body of occult ideas formulated earlier in
this century by Rudolf Steiner (1861-1925). Steiner, the leading
German figure in the nineteenth-century esoteric "wisdom"
cult Theosophy, founded the German Theosophical Society;
he went on to found his own doctrine, Anthroposophy, and the
Anthroposophical Society thereafter. He wrote many books on
his occult spiritualistic philosophy.

Anthroposophy holds a particular attraction in the German
counterculture today, as it did in the *völkisch* movement of
the 1920s. The Waldorf schools, for example, were founded
on Steiner's educational principles and are respectable in
many German and American countercultural circles. (There
are more than sixty in the Federal Republic today.) Founded
by Steiner in 1920, they provide children with an alternative,
reformed education, one that is free from aggression and
from pressures to achieve, one that places emphasis on the
musical aspects of life and on feelings over understanding.
Steiner is also the founder of biodynamic farming, a form
of organic agriculture that does without pesticides and tries
to foster a more organic relationship between cultivator
and soil. Biodynamic agriculturists today produce a line of

organic foods under the brand name Demeter and a line of cosmetics under the name Weleda. Many people have been and continue to be innocently attracted to these efforts and to Anthroposophy without any notion of the less savory aspects of Steiner's work.

Yet not all of Steiner's beliefs were benignly ecospiritual. For one thing, Anthroposophy classifies humanity into "root races" in an esoteric evolutionary theory.[24] Building on a similar doctrine in Theosophy, the root-race theory is integral to Anthroposophy's cosmology. According to this doctrine, a series of root races of human beings evolved sequentially over the millennia, each superior to the ones that preceded it, each with a higher level of development of self-consciousness. The first two root races, the Polar and Hyperborean, were "astral-etheric"; they are now extinct—the evolutionary process superseded them. The next people to evolve were a bit higher, but they were still half animal, purely instinctive, lacking the capacity for conceptual thought and memory. The fourth root race finally began to be recognizably human; finally came the Atlantans, to which Europeans belong. The European whites, as the most highly developed so far, are at the summit of the hierarchical scale of humanity; they have brought everything that is good to humanity, since they "are the only ones who have developed humanity within themselves."[25] These various races have been mostly killed off in various catastrophes of one kind or another, after which only certain people—presumably the fittest—survived; "in the case of the inferior kinds of human beings," wrote Steiner, " ... the life body was not sufficiently protected to enable it to withstand the Luciferic influence."[26] There are numerous subdivisions within these basic root races. Blacks, for example, must live in Africa, we learn, a land of much heat and light; blacks soak up this heat and light, and their brains are specially constructed to process it; their supposed highly instinctual nature results from all this processing.

> And since the sun, light, and heat are retained in his epidermis, [the black's] whole metabolism proceeds as if he were being cooked inside himself by the sun. From this results his instinctive life. Within the black, he is continuously being cooked, and what stokes this fire is his posterior brain.[27]

Once blacks emigrate out of Africa, the balance of light and heat is different, and therefore they will die out—"they are in fact a declining race, they will die out of their own nature, since they are receiving too little light and heat."[28] Such a theory would justify accelerating the extinction of races since they are presumably going to die off anyway. In the future, wrote Steiner in 1909, certain people who have not reached a "high level of development" will incline toward evil: "The laggard souls will have accumulated in their karma so much error, ugliness, and evil that there will form, for the time being, a special union of evil and aberrant human beings who voluntarily oppose the community of good men."[29]

Perhaps this root-race theory was what appealed to Rudolf Hess about Anthroposophy, for he became an Anthroposophist. As Ditfurth points out, "The root-race ideology of the Theosophists and the Anthroposophists melded seamlessly into the National Socialist idea of the purity of the 'Aryan race.'"[30] Certainly Steiner's ideas on biodynamic farming influenced some National Socialists. Anthroposophical ideas are eminently usable by ecofascists today, and there is a strong right wing within the Anthroposophists that is closely connected with the ultra-right. Author Günther Bartsch is an Anthroposophist who is also a National Revolutionary of the Solidarist variety; the author of an adulatory 1989 biography of Otto Strasser, he attempts in his publications to synthesize ecological themes based on Steiner's ideas with Strasser's political ideas.[31] It should be noted that Anthroposophy is also well funded by huge multinational corporations like Siemens and Bertelsmann.[32]

Among the ultra-right adherents of Anthroposophy today are officials of the World League for the Protection of Life (WSL), a small but influential and very wealthy environmental organization in the Federal Republic. The garden at its educational center is cultivated according to biodynamic methods, and visitors are served organic refreshments. Yet this organization was founded in 1958 by former members of the National Socialist party, and today it links protection of "life" (that is, "right-to-life") themes and the environment with racism and a revival of *völkisch* ideology. The "life" it is most interested in protecting is of course German "life"; thus the WSL is rabidly anti-abortion, believing that German women should be devoted to giving birth to "Aryan" babies.

The spiritual leader of the WSL and its key figure for most of its history has been Werner Georg Haverbeck. Born in 1909, Haverbeck became an active Nazi at an early age; it should be recalled that Nazism was largely a youth movement, so that members like Haverbeck are still alive.[33] Haverbeck joined the SA in 1928 and from 1929 to 1932 was a member of the Reich Administration for the National Socialist Student League (Reichsleitung der NSDAP-Studentenschaft) and a leader of the Reich Youth Leadership of the Hitler Youth (Reichjugendführung der Hitlerjugend). He served as a leading official of the Strength Through Joy organization, which controlled recreational activities under the Third Reich; in 1933 Rudolf Hess saw to it that Haverbeck's passport was stamped "This man is not to be arrested." He survived the Röhm purge to help organize the Nuremberg Party Congress and join Hess's staff. It was Hess who converted him to Anthroposophy. During the war he conducted radio propaganda in Denmark and worked in South America; by the end of the war he was an officer.[34]

After the Allies rudely aborted Haverbeck's many efforts on behalf of the Third Reich, he contented himself for a time working as a pastor for the Anthroposophical Christian community. He founded an educational center called the Collegium Humanum in 1963, where today ecofascist, esoteric, *völkisch*, Anthroposophist, neopagan, and primitivist groups meet and hold workshops. He co-founded the WSL and served as its president from 1974 to 1982. In 1981, he was a signatory of the notorious Heidelberg Manifesto, a document drawn up by a group of professors to warn the German people of the dangers that immigration posed to them. Its first draft began:

> With great concern we observe the subversion of the German people through the influx of many millions of foreigners and their families, the foreignization of our language, our culture, and our nationhood … . Already many Germans have become

> foreigners in their living districts and workplaces, and thus in
> their own *Heimat*.[35]

Routine as this language may sound now, when opposition to immigration in the Federal Republic is much more tolerated and neofascists pander to it relentlessly, the Manifesto had to be toned down at the time (1981) because of the public outcry it raised.

In accordance with Anthroposophical root-race beliefs, Haverbeck is notable for propounding the thesis that the two world wars in this century in fact constituted a thirty years' war waged by foreign aggressors against the German people and their spiritual life. Apparently, German spiritual life stood in the way of "the strivings for world domination by the Anglo-Saxon race," behind which lay "the intensive image of a call to world dominance, like the old Jewish consciousness." Indeed, Haverbeck maintains, the two world wars amounted to a conspiracy against the German people and spiritual life. It is a "historical lie" that the Nazis ran "mass-murder camps," argues Haverbeck, and is actually "enemy propaganda." It was Russia that was the aggressor in the Second World War.[36]

In his 1989 book *Rudolf Steiner: Advocate for Germany*, Haverbeck lauds Steiner (who died in 1925) for understanding the existence of this ongoing conspiracy early on.

> During the First World War Rudolf Steiner delivered a
> multitude of lectures about contemporary history, and he toiled
> inexhaustibly for the truth about the question of "war guilt." ...
> Steiner presented his listeners with maps that showed that goals
> that had been proclaimed back in 1889 were being fulfilled

[during World War I]. These maps anticipated the separation of Central Europe that would be ultimately achieved with the loss of East Germany … . What was not fully achieved through the Versailles treaty in 1919 was in fact completed in 1945: the demolition of Germany … . The leading forces of both parties to the cold war were united in this common struggle against spiritual Germany. "This war [World War I] was a conspiracy against German spiritual life," said Steiner.[37]

When Haverbeck's book on Steiner's nationalism was published, it caused an outcry of protest among outraged countercultural Anthroposophists who send their children to Waldorf Schools, use Demeter products, and are in no way racists or fascists. Yet as researcher Wölk points out, their protests were unwarranted, since Haverbeck was only presenting Steiner as what he actually was—"a crude nationalist whose demonizations were shared by the *völkisch* groups of his day"—to show his usefulness for nationalist and neofascist groups today.[38]

This alleged conspiracy against German spiritual life pervades much of the WSL's current thinking, notes Wölk. WSLers consider the "flood of asylum-seekers," the destruction of the environment, and the ongoing transformation of the Federal Republic into a multicultural society to be part of the spiritual war against the Germans. They regard the protection of the environment as part of the protection of a people, of its biological "substance" and its national identity. Indeed, WSLers see the battle for a healthy environment as part of the all-encompassing spiritual struggle against the homogenizing forces of modernity and "Western civilization." Haverbeck's wife, Ursula Haverbeck-Wetzel, another former WSL president who "for religious reasons refuses to dissociate herself from any human being, including Adolf Hitler,"[39] observes:

> Whenever a person comes to feel that he belongs to the cultural strain that is deeply rooted in his people which has not only a material existence but a spiritual reality that is superior to the material plane—he has broken out from being a manipulated consumer. He has escaped the mass homogenization of completely manipulated people who are "amusing themselves to death" (as Neil Postman put it), which is the goal of "One World" advocates, intent on power and domination. The person who is faithful to his religious convictions and attentive and caring to his culture and customs, they consider dangerous.[40]

Ernst Otto Cohrs, the WSL's president since 1989, is another devotee of Rudolf Steiner, having been an Anthroposophist since 1961. Today Cohrs's interests seem to lie in promulgating race theories, and publishing and distributing anti-Semitic literature. In 1982, an official of the WSL's Bavarian chapter made a public issue of Cohrs's activities inside the WSL. He wrote a letter to a WSL membership assembly saying that it should dissociate itself from Cohrs because, among other things, he was sending anti-Semitic literature to WSL members, running advertisements in ultra-right magazines like *Bauernschaft* (the journal of the notorious Holocaust-denier Thies Christophersen), permitting neofascist periodicals to reprint WSL leaflets, and himself distributing such writings as *There Were No Gas Chambers and The Auschwitz Myth*.[41] Many members withdrew from the WSL as a result of this letter; those who remained were overwhelmingly those who shared Cohrs's anti-Semitic ideas and were not disposed to contradict him. Among them was Baldur Springmann, the "ecofarmer" who was involved in the Greens in the early days, whose book *Partner Erde* (Partner Earth) was published by an ultra-right publisher (Arndt Verlag), and who writes for the "New" Right publication *Nation Europa*; and Dr. Arnold Neugebohrn, a Republican candidate for the provincial legislature who takes pride in his NSDAP "gold medal." Concludes Wölk, "The internal crisis caused by Cohrs's activities in 1981-82 may have diminished the ranks of the WSL, but it also strengthened the WSL's neofascist orientation." Cohrs's current activities are still primarily the dissemination of Holocaust-denial literature.[42]

One collective member of the WSL is a Hamburg-based organization known as the Society for Biological Anthropology, Eugenics, and Behavioral Research (Gesellschaft für biologische Anthropologie, Eugenik, und Verhaltensforschung, or GfbAEV), whose head is Jürgen Rieger, a "neo-Nazi in lawyer's robes" (as the newspaper *Die Zeit* called him) who is currently defending two fascist groups that the Federal Republic banned in 1992; one of the GfbAEV's fellows is the leading ideologue of the French Nouvelle Droite, Alain de Benoist. Its periodical is the notorious quarterly journal *Neue Anthropologie*, which maintains, among other things, that there has always been environmental destruction in the history of humanity, that in fact one could even say this was part of human nature were it not for one sole exception:

Only the Germans were different. In pagan times they worshipped groves and trees, and because of their closeness to nature, they had a caring orientation toward nature. Even the love of animals is much more pronounced among the Germanic peoples than it is, for example, among the Romance-language-speaking peoples. It is thus no coincidence that even today the most stalwart environmentalist efforts—private as well as state—are those conducted by peoples who have a larger proportion of the Nordic race.[43]

Rudolf Bahro: *Völkisch* Spirituality

If fascists are using ecological themes to update their racial and nationalist aims, other thinkers are developing an ecological spiritualism along New Age lines that bears no small resemblance to the *völkisch* Germanic spirituality of the 1920s. Indeed, "a great part of the literature about close-to-nature spirituality that the alternative scene is reading is permeated with reactionary, *völkisch*, or even National Socialist content," writes Ditfurth. "We find neofascist and ultra-right positions not only in the various political and even ecological groups, but also … in neopagan, esoteric and occult circles."[44]

Perhaps the most prominent figure in this connection is Rudolf Bahro. Many German "new social movement" circles previously accepted Bahro as a social theorist contributing to a "socialism with a human face" and continue to regard him as part of the independent left; leftist periodicals publish uncritical interviews with him. In the Anglo-American world, too, many ecological radicals still consider Bahro as representing something "leftist." Yet Bahro no longer considers himself a leftist; indeed, he is a vehement critic of the left[45] and of "comrades without fatherland."[46] In fact, as antifascist researcher Roger Niedenführ argues, since the mid-1980s Bahro has been contributing to the development of a "spiritual fascism" that has the effect of "rehabilitating National Socialism," openly calling for reclaiming the "positive" side of the Nazi movement. [47] Not only does Bahro appeal to a mystical Germanist spirituality like the *völkisch* ideologues of the 1920s, he even sees the need for a "Green Adolf" who will lead Germans out of their own "folk-depths" and into ecological "salvation."

Bahro originally became well known as the author of *The Alternative in Eastern Europe*, which he wrote during the 1970s while he was a dissident Marxist and party member in the former East Germany. In 1977, the ruling Communist government sentenced him to prison; in 1979, he was deported. Once arrived in what was then West Germany, Bahro became involved with the nascent German Greens, affirming that "red and green go well together."[48] In the early 1980s peace movement, he alarmed many by enunciating nationalistic arguments against the deployment of Pershing missiles.[49] He began to speak less in political terms and more in religious terms, asking that "the emphasis [be] shifted from politics and the question of power towards the cultural level ... to the prophetic level ... . Our aim has to be the 'reconstruction of God.'"[50] He became a vocal "fundamentalist" critic of the *realo* wing of the Greens (those who became generally committed to exercising parliamentary power) and ultimately left the party in 1985. In a parting speech in Hamburg, he said there were structural similarities between the Greens and the

Nazi movement that the Greens were not taking advantage of but should; then he gave his "fundamentalist" alternative: "the other republic that we want will be an association of communities of life-communities in which God and Goddess are at the center."[51]

Bahro thereafter moved increasingly toward the New Age esoteric milieu. His major concern remained "the ecological crisis," whose "deep structures" must be investigated, but he now thinks ecology "has nothing to do with left and right."[52] Today Bahro is one of the leading spokespeople and theorists of New Age ideas in the Federal Republic. "The most important thing," he rambles,

> is that ... [people] take the path "back" and align themselves with the Great Equilibrium, in the harmony between the human order and the Tao of life. I think the "esoteric"-political theme of "king and queen of the world" is basically the question of how men and women are to comprehend and interact with each other in a spiritually comprehensive way. Whoever does not bring themselves to cooperate with the world government [*Weltregierung*] will get their due.[53]

In 1989, Bahro cofounded a combination educational center and commune near Trier, the Lernwerkstatt (an "ecological academy for one world"), whose purpose is to synthesize spirituality and politics, "to come to a new personal and social orientation." It presents lectures, cultural events, and weekend workshops on various New Age themes, including deep ecology, ecofeminism, Zen Buddhism, holistic nutrition, Sufism, and the like—as well as German identity.[54] His 1987 book *Logik der*

Rettung marked an overt embrace of authoritarian theological concepts that shocked many former admirers.[55]

Bahro also holds a professorship at Humboldt University in Berlin, where he conducts a seminar whose sessions are usually filled to overflowing. At Humboldt, he holds a chair in "social ecology," and he refers to his "science" by this name, but Bahro's work is not to be confused with the social ecology conceived and developed by Murray Bookchin. Although the two theorists agree that class contradictions are not the exclusive social contradiction, Bookchin regards hierarchy as basic, while emphasizing the importance of class interests. Bahro, by contrast, points to "tribal consciousness" as rooted "more deeply than class consciousness," even in the spiritually "deepest layers" of a people. "The national question is an objective reality," Bahro says, that is on a much "deeper basis than the class question."[56]

Moreover, whereas Bookchin's consistently internationalist social ecology affirms reason and naturalism and repeatedly criticizes ecomysticism and ecotheology, Bahro's version of "social ecology" is overwhelmingly spiritualistic. Indeed, in late 1990, when Bookchin spoke at the Humboldt seminar at Bahro's invitation, Bahro told Bookchin that his (Bahro's) own "social ecology" was actually an attempt to synthesize Bookchin's social ecology with deep ecology.[57] Politics must be based on spiritualistic values today, in Bahro's view, because "without a return to the spiritual source," politics "will not be worthy of that name."[58] Not only are those who see spirituality and politics as opposites fundamentally wrong, he argues, but our global ecological problems are in fact a material reflection of the inner spiritual "sickness" that separates them. It is a religious "politics of consciousness"—that is, the implanting of spiritualistic ideas—that can arrest the global ecological crisis and prepare people for the new political order.[59]

Bahro's spiritualistic approach has a distinctly ethno-cultural dimension. He speaks of peoples as if they had unique spiritual "essences" that are indissoluble, that cannot be destroyed over time.[60] He is particularly concerned with the "German essence" (*deutsche Wesenheit*) and its various manifestations on the material plane.[61] In approaching the ecological crisis, the German "essence" demands the incorporation of spiritualism, particularly the mystical tradition initiated by Meister Eckhart, whom "we Germans should read."[62] Bahro favorably contrasts this "German legacy"[63] with socialism and the Enlightenment.

It appears not to alarm Bahro, as antifascist researcher Peter Kratz points out, that his mystical Germanism closely resembles the mystical Germanism of the *völkisch* movement.[64] Bahro, in fact, consciously associates himself with the *völkisch* movement—he says he wants an "awakening in the *Volk*"[65]— and with the 1920s Conservative Revolution against the Enlightenment generally.[66] Indeed, Bahro is critical of the Greens, among other things, because they did "not attend to this *völkisch* moment."[67] Kratz warns that this gives Bahro's approach "the same potential for political catastrophe that the *völkisch* movement had, even though this would please Bahro as little as it would have pleased the originators of the *völkisch* movement."[68]

"Essences" like the "German essence" cannot remain in the spiritual plane; they must be manifested in concrete reality—that is, in politics, history, and society. In Bahro's prospectus (and in stark contrast to Bookchin's anarchist libertarian municipalism), these manifestations will not take the form of democratic institutions, since "to say that we will create grassroots democracy now, among these wolves, is nonsense."[69] Bahro criticizes the "bean-counting voting" process of democracy and prefers a spiritual consensus process for decision making.[70] Although he is currently receiving state support from Saxony for an eco-communal demonstration project (thanks largely to his friend and visiting lecturer at Humboldt, Saxon prime minister Kurt Biedenkopf), Bahro also rejects the state: "society's rule of law," he asserts, "may no longer be based on the state or on any other existing forces that are even less legitimate."[71]

Despite his antistatist assertions, which may make him appear attractively anti-authoritarian, like many "New" Rightists Bahro expressly believes that the ecological crisis is resolvable only through authoritarian means. He calls for a spiritually based and hierarchically elitist "salvation government" (*Rettungsregierung*) or a "god-state" (*Gottesstaat*)[72] that will be run by a "new political authority at the highest level": a "prince of the ecological turn."[73] The "prince," which apparently may be a collective entity, will constitute a spiritual elite, an oligarchy responsible only to God. As a "voice of the divine,"[74] this guru elite will dictate the law of God and nature, in order to convert the present society to the "order according to nature"[75] that Bahro sees as desirable. People should not "be afraid" of the advent of this "prince," says Bahro, since "a bit of 'ecodictatorship' is needed" to handle our problems today.[76] Besides, "it is a matter of absolute indifference whether [this prince] is a man or a woman," he assures us, "it is a question of structure. That is the German moment in this Green movement."[77] But today it is important to develop a broad spiritual consciousness in the general population, for "without a spiritual determination, there will be no new redemptive institutionalization"—that is, no "prince."[78] It is presumably cheering that "in spite of all bad experiences ... the strongest political-psychological dispositions of our people" make "the Germans more responsive than other peoples to charismatic leadership."[79]

Liberating the "Brown Parts"

Since the mid-1980s, Bahro has been remarkably open about proclaiming his embrace of the spiritual content of fascism for the "salvation" of nature and humanity. In *The Logic of Salvation*, he asks, "Is there really no thought more reprehensible than a new 1933?"—that is, Hitler's rise to state power. "But that is precisely what can save us! The ecology and peace movement is the first popular German movement since the Nazi movement. It must co-redeem [*miterlösen*] Hitler."[80] Indeed, "the Nazi movement [was] among other things an early reading of the ecology movement."[81] Germans are to look for "the positive that may lie buried in the Nazi movement" and reclaim it, he says, "because if we do not, we will remain cut off from our roots, the roots from which will grow that which will save us."[82] Today one must "liberate" the "brown parts" in the German character.[83] The fact is, says Bahro, that today "there is a call in the depths of the *Volk* for a Green Adolf."[84]

When Bahro's critics reproach him for this assertion, Bahro responds that no, he does not mean Adolf *Hitler*. That his leftist critics think he means Adolf *Hitler* shows that the left "responds only with fear, instead of comprehending that a Green Adolf would be an entirely different Adolf from the one we know about."[85] Yet as Kratz points out, Bahro himself is evasive about what this "Green Adolf" actually would be: perhaps a personified *Führer*, perhaps a spiritual elite, or perhaps some inner self-recognition that within each of us there is supposedly a "Green Adolf," to whom we must subordinate ourselves voluntarily through spiritual insight. This evasiveness is itself a matter of concern. Kratz believes that Bahro really means a personified *Führer*; for one thing, Bahro invokes the "sleeping emperor" myth,[86] the nationalistic notion that the Emperor Barbarossa is sleeping in the Kyffhäuser Mountain and will one day come back as the *Führer* and rescue Germany from dire straits[87]—an idea that is also one of the foundations of the Nazi *Führer* principle.

For Bahro, this *Führer* will clearly be a spiritualistic leader. In a foreword to a book by his colleague Jochen Kirchhoff, he argued that National Socialism had had the right spiritual aims: it sought to manifest the "German essence" on the material plane. It went wrong in the execution—for one thing, it was very violent. But even this was understandable since, arising as it did in the 1920s, it was the task of National Socialism to make the first real spiritual revolt against the overwhelming materialism of the age. Thus, the materialistic thinking of the Weimar era, against which National Socialism rebelled, was the real cause of the Nazis" material "vehemence"—that is, mass murder.[88]

The materialistic thinking of Weimar modernity that the Nazis were so correct to oppose, says Bahro, is also today the immediate cause of the ecological crisis. Only the spiritualization of consciousness, Bahro believes, can prevail over biosphere-destroying materialism. Hence Germans today have no alternative but to invoke the spiritually "deep forces" from the Nazi movement—in order to "be present with our whole potential."[89]

But it must be a strictly spiritual endeavor: undertaking concrete political resistance on the material plane is, for Bahro, itself an integral component of materialistic secularism, an expression of negative spirituality. Those who engage in politics on the material plane today, he says, in fact politically resemble—Nazis! True, the Nazis had to struggle in the twenties, but at least they had the right spiritual ideas. But "revolt (under the conditions of our imperial situation) is fascistic. That is to say, it redeems [*rettet*] nothing."[90] Bahro's religious dispensation thus does not synthesize spirituality and politics at all, as critic Niedenführ points out; on the contrary, it simply eliminates political action.[91]

Repelled by these ideas, critics have denounced *The Logic of Salvation* as fascistic or "fascistoid"—potentially fascist. Bahro responds that such "faint-hearted antifascism" has "refused" to "look for the strength that lay beneath the brown movement."[92] Precisely because the left rejects the insights of spirituality, it can never see the necessity of *völkisch*-authoritarian structures and therefore can never give material form to the "German essence," he believes. Bahro replied further in his next book, *Rückkehr*:

> It can be instructive that there was a strong wing of the Nazis that wanted to be socially and culturally revolutionary. This wing was not consolidated, and the Hitler movement went

on to serve a regenerated German capitalism ... . We can no
longer allow fascism to be a taboo subject.

It should be noted that fascism has hardly been a "taboo
subject" in the Federal Republic—on the contrary, it has been
much discussed. What has been rightly rejected—and hardly
merely "taboo," since a taboo begs to be broken—is sympathy
for the Nazis. Bahro continues:

> I can't rule out the possibility that at the end of the 1920s I
> wouldn't have gone with the Nazis. And it's very important that
> we be prepared to ask such a question. As for what would have
> happened later, I don't know. There were people in the Nazi
> movement who gave it up before 1933; there were people who
> saw the light with the Röhm affair; some went into the resistance;
> others were executed. But we're not supposed to imagine what we
> ourselves would have done. And I was ready and am ready to go
> into such questions. I think that if we are serious about forming
> a popular movement and overcoming the ecological crisis, and
> if we are really to address what comes out of the depths, we will
> have to have a lot to do with what it was that found expression
> then and that is seeking another, better expression this time. That
> can go well only if there is a great deal of consciousness about
> whatever unhappy mechanisms lie in all of us, the resentment
> reactions, mere rebellion instead of revolution.[93]

Posing as a courageous inquiry into the breaking of taboos,
such practices do nothing more than give people permission
to envision themselves as Nazis—a horrifying dispensation
in any era, but particularly in one when present-day Nazis

75

routinely attack foreigners in German towns and cities and when fascist parties are having electoral victories.

Some of Bahro's associates add to the strong suspicion that his "Green Adolf" refers to a new *Führer*. One of his fellow teachers at the Lernwerkstatt, for example, is Rainer Langhans, a former anarchistic "wild man" of the 1960s German student organization SDS who writes today that "spirituality in Germany is named Hitler. And only when you have gone a little bit further can you go beyond it. Until then, however, you must reclaim the inheritance ... not in the sense of this fine exclusionary antifascism but in the sense of further developing what Hitler tried to do." And: "This dumb Enlightenment, which builds up dams against so-called 'outbreaks of the irrational,' is actually merely laughable as an antifascist syndrome." And: "We have to be, so to speak, the better fascists."[94] Another of Bahro's fellow teachers at the Lernwerkstatt is Jochen Kirchhoff, who writes that "National Socialism was a botched attempt at healing the world ... and to ground politics in the spiritual."[95]

To speak at his seminar at Humboldt, Bahro also invited Wolfgang Deppert, a onetime head of the *völkisch*-racist sect German Unitary Religion Community (DUR), even though at the end of 1990 Deppert permitted the publication in one of his periodicals of an article by Princess Marie-Adelheid Reuss-zur-Lippe. Earlier in her life, in the 1920s, this person was a founder of the "Nordic Ring" and later a close political and personal confidante of the Third Reich's Agriculture Minister, Walther Darré, who called her "my little sister." In 1985, she was the editor-in-chief of the journal *Bauernschaft (Peasantry)*, whose publisher is Thies Christophersen, the notorious author of the despicable 1973 pamphlet *Die Auschwitz Lüge (The Auschwitz Lie)*.[96] Deppert, apparently, spoke at the Humboldt seminar on philosophy and science.

But whatever happened at that lecture, Murray Bookchin's appearance at the seminar on November 21, 1990, did not go over well with the host. Bahro had asked Bookchin to address such questions as "Is the alternative to ecological destruction freedom from domination or an 'ecological' dictatorship?" Bookchin replied that "an "ecological" dictatorship would not be ecological—it would finally finish off the planet altogether. It would be the glorification, the hypostasization, of social control, of manipulation, the objectification of human beings, the denial of human freedom and self-consciousness, in the name of ecological problems. ... An 'ecological' dictatorship is a contradiction in terms, an oxymoron."

When Bookchin had finished his presentation, the following exchange took place:

> **Bahro:** You put such a spotlight on the positive side of human nature—cooperation and so on—that if that were true, it's improbable that again and again we would have fallen back into egotism and competition. You see human nature predominantly as positive. But more often than not, it has worked out for the worse rather than for the better. Most often the institutions that the human species has created have had hierarchy and domination. The fact that they did so must have a foundation in human nature. ...
>
> When you talk about rationality, *Geist,* the fully developed capacity of being human, you are confronting this side least—

the "dark side." Because that is what gives us the capacity to dominate, this *Geist,* our rationality. You don't want to confront that as fundamental. ...

Bookchin: I don't ignore the "dark side" of humanity ... But if the "dark side" exists everywhere, then why has it been necessary for the "dark side" to express itself in institutions of the most barbarous kind? Why did there have to be coercion? Why does that "dark side" always have to be institutionalized through force, through superstition, through fear, through threat, and through ideologies of the most barbarous nature? ... There's no question that there is a "dark side" to human history. ... But it's very hard to find the biological reasons for that "dark side." Because that "dark side" has always operated through the institutions of a minority who relied on force and depended on propaganda and superstition, and on the worst things that the human mind can develop, to suppress the millions and millions.

Bahro: But does it have natural foundations?

Bookchin: It emerges from a social foundation ... . If the "dark side" is natural, why is it that in all the great revolutions that we know of, people have broken out with a generosity of spirit that is incredible? They have been willing to trust, to care, to feel the pain even of their masters—when their masters tried to oppress them, owing to their own insecurities. ... In warrior societies, to make the adolescent transformation into a warrior, you have to inflict pain upon him. You have to spoil him, to make him a sufferer in order to make him part of the

community of warriors. ... I don't see the "dark side" of human
nature, but of social nature.[97]

After Bookchin gave his lecture, Bahro told Bookchin that he
would not invite him to speak again.

Social Darwinist "Ecology": Herbert Gruhl

Bahro, let it be said, claims to look for the roots of the ecological
crisis in the "sickness" in "white Nordic humanity." But the far
right most often locates these roots in non-Europeans and uses
"ecology" to marshal classic racist arguments against Third
World immigration. In the "Europe of fatherlands" of the
"ethnopluralism" concept, each *Volk* requires its own specific,
familiar home environment in order to thrive. Interference
from outside—including immigration—disturbs that natural
environment, the "natural ecology of the *Volk*." Most often, the
far right claims to be defending cultures rather than races; if
the Nazis persecuted those who practiced "*race* mixing" and
sought to preserve "*racial* purity," today's fascists say they
oppose *cultural* mixing and seek to preserve their *culture*. Thus,
the ecofascist and misleadingly named Ecological Democratic
Party (Ökologische Demokratische Partei, or ÖDP) calls for
"asylum-seekers [to] be accepted by countries that belong to
the same *cultural* area as the asylum seekers themselves," and
they call for "*Heimat* instead of multiculture."[98]

The hollowness of such claims becomes evident, however,
when they are clothed in terms of "ecology." For the far
right's notion of ecology is in fact nothing more than social
Darwinism, the reactionary ideology that biology dictates the

form of society, that genes rather than environment determine culture. Social Darwinist "ecology" can then advance seemingly "ecological" reasons for keeping out immigrants and for asserting ethnic or national identity—while avoiding the terminology of race.

Social Darwinism has deep roots in the German ultra-right. When it first emerged as a doctrine in the nineteenth century, its German form was very different from its Anglo-American form. Like Anglo-American social Darwinism, German social Darwinism projected human social institutions onto the nonhuman world as "natural laws," then invoked those "laws" to justify the human social arrangements as "natural." It also applied the maxim "survival of the fittest" to society. But where Anglo-American social Darwinism conceived the "fittest" as the individual entrepreneur in a "bloody tooth and claw" capitalist jungle, German social Darwinism overwhelmingly conceived the "fittest" in terms of race. Thus, the "fittest" race not only would but should survive, vanquishing all its competitors in its "struggle for existence." As historian Daniel Gasman observes:

> It may be said that if Darwinism in England was an extension of *laissez faire* individualism projected from the social world to the natural world, [in Germany it was] a projection of German romanticism and philosophical idealism. ... The form which social Darwinism took in Germany was a pseudo-scientific religion of nature worship and nature-mysticism combined with notions of racism.[99]

Since this social Darwinism seemed to give a "scientific" basis to racism, National Socialism drew heavily on it to provide "scientific" grounds for its virulent racism. Hitler wrote in *Mein Kampf*, for example, that people "owe their higher existence, not to the ideas of a few crazy ideologists, but to the knowledge and ruthless application of Nature's stern and rigid laws." Among these "laws": "Nature usually makes certain corrective decisions with regard to the racial purity of earthly creatures. She has little love for bastards."[100] To establish their totalitarian regime and implement genocide, the Nazis easily drew on the common ideology that the *Volk* mediates between individual and cosmos, rendering the individual mainly a member of a larger whole, the "*Volk* whole" or "*Volk* community."

It is well known among ecological activists today that Ernst Haeckel coined the term *ecology* in the 1860s; what is less known is that Haeckel was the primary spokesperson for German social Darwinism in the latter half of the nineteenth century, as Gasman shows. German social Darwinism was thus almost immediately married to the concept of ecology. Haeckel was also a believer in mystical racism and nationalism, so that German social Darwinism was from the beginning a political concept that lent romantic racism and nationalism a pseudo-biological basis. In fact, as Gasman argues,

> racially inspired social Darwinism in Germany … was almost completely indebted to Haeckel for its creation … . His ideas served to unite into a full-bodied ideology the trends of racism, imperialism, romanticism, anti-Semitism and nationalism …
> . It was Haeckel who brought the full weight of science down hard on the side of what were Volkism's essentially irrational and mystical ideas.[101]

Haeckel himself was a proponent of carrying over concepts like "selective breeding" and "racial hygiene" from nonhuman nature into human society.

Despite the widely different scientific concepts of ecology that have emerged since Haeckel's day, the "ecology" that today's ecofascists draw upon is essentially the social Darwinism of Haeckel. Perhaps the most prominent social Darwinist-"ecological" racist in Germany today is Herbert Gruhl,[102] a former Christian Democrat parliamentarian whose best-selling 1975 book, *A Planet Is Plundered: The Balance of Terror of Our Politics,* makes an explicit social Darwinist interpretation of ecology.[103] In the late 1970s and early 1980s Gruhl participated in the formation of the German Greens with a new political group he had founded, Green Action Future (GAZ). It was Gruhl who created the slogan "We are neither left nor right; we are in front," according to Charlene Spretnak and Fritjof Capra.[104] In the early 1980s, ultrarightists, including Gruhl's GAZ, struggled with leftists and centrists for the direction of the Green Party; the center-left ultimately took control. "It is to the credit of the leftist tendencies in the founding phases of the Greens," writes Ditfurth, "that the ultra-right and neofascists were prevented from taking over ecological politics, as they were threatening to do at the time."[105]

Gruhl, on the losing end, concluded that the Greens had given up their "concern for ecology in favor of a leftist ideology of emancipation" and walked out of the party. He continued his fight for his conception of ecology outside the Greens, however; with his fellow ultra-rightist Baldur Springmann, he founded the Ecological Democratic Party (ÖDP) in 1982 and wrote most of its programmatic literature, orienting ecology toward fascism and endowing racism and population policy with an "ecological" legitimation. In 1989, when an ÖDP party congress dared to pass a resolution formally distancing the party from the NPD and the Republicans, this "leftist victory" was too much for Gruhl, and he left to form yet another group. Since the mid-1980s, Gruhl has appeared as a guest speaker at various neo-Nazi and Holocaust-denial events[106] and continues to publish books on "ecology."

Gruhl's social Darwinist "ecology" reduces human beings to their biological attributes and applies the "laws" of nature to society: "All laws that apply to living nature generally apply to people as well, since people themselves are part of living nature," he maintains.[107] These "natural laws" dictate that people should accept the present social order as it is. Domination, hierarchy, and exploitation should be accepted, since "the swan is white, without anyone artificially cleaning it. The raven is black, and everything is in its natural place of its own accord. This is good. All the strivings of people … for organized justice are simply hopeless."[108] People should adapt to existing conditions instead of making futile attempts to change them, since "every life-form accommodates itself to that which it cannot change."[109]

If society were set up according to nature, Gruhl believes, cultures would institute prescriptions against those who deviate from their existing norms, since "in the hunting grounds of the wilderness, if an animal breaks the unwritten law of the herd and goes its own way, it generally pays for this independence with its life."[110] Moreover, cultures should be kept separate from one another: "When many cultures are all jumbled together in the same area, the result will be that they live alongside each other, in conflict with each other, or …

they will undergo entropy, becoming a mixture whose value lessens with every intermixing, until in the last analysis it has no more worth." The reason for cultural separation too has its basis in "natural law," "a law of entropy which we particularly have in ecology, and this law also holds for human cultures."[111]

In the coming years, Gruhl believes that cultures around the globe will compete for survival over the means of life, in a social Darwinist struggle for existence. "There is no doubt that the wars of the future will be fought over shares in the basic foundations of life—that is, over the basis of nutrition and the increasingly precious fruits of the soil. Under these circumstances, future wars will far surpass in frightfulness all previous wars."[112] The peoples who have the best prospects for survival will be those who are best armed and who best conserve their resources; those who "succeed in bringing their military preparedness to the highest level, while keeping their standard of living low, will have an enormous advantage."[113]

In the interests of this struggle, Germans must not only arm themselves but preserve their environment by keeping the number of people who inhabit it down: "Violations of ecological equilibrium and the destruction of natural living spaces [*Lebensräume*] are directly related to population density."[114]

"Overpopulation" in the Third World, however, has produced "armies of job-seekers" who are entering Germany with a "capacity for annihilation" comparable to a "nuclear bomb," Gruhl writes. This "tidal wave of humanity" is a primary menace that will cause "all order to break down" in Europe. Third World immigrants are thus threatening European culture itself, which will "perish not because of the degeneration of its own people, as previous high civilizations have, but because of physical laws: the constantly overflowing mass of humanity on an earth's surface that remains constant."[115] Therefore, there is no room for immigrants in the Federal Republic: "Because of its high population density, the Federal Republic of Germany, one of the most densely settled countries on earth, cannot be a destination country for immigrants. We therefore reject the unlimited acceptance of foreigners."[116] Accordingly, Gruhl demands "an end to immigration for ecological reasons."[117]

The "laws of nature," for Gruhl, offer a solution to Third World immigration, especially the "law" that "the only acceptable currency with which violations of natural law can be paid for is death. Death brings the equalization; it cuts back all life that has overgrown on this planet, so that the planet can once again come into equilibrium." [118] Fortunately, in his view, Third World people will accept this lethal solution since their lives "rest on a completely different basic outlook on life from our own: their own death, like that of their children, is accepted as fate."[119]

Needless to say, Gruhl does not think democracy is the most efficient way to address these problems. After all, this situation "will take on the proportions of an emergency in coming years, and attempts that will be made to prevail in it will produce a permanent state of emergency."[120] In an interview with the editors of *Junge Freiheit (Young Freedom),* the flagship publication of the National Revolutionaries, Gruhl was asked whether the problems of protecting the environment and life can be solved within a democracy. "Probably not," he replied, "because democracies follow the Zeitgeist, and in all countries of the world today the Zeitgeist is to raise the standard of living further. Parties that warn about this and advocate renunciation of consumption seem to have little chance." Instead, Gruhl demands a "strong state," strong both internationally and domestically—if possible, even a state with "dictatorial powers."[121]

In the autumn of 1991, the environmental minister of Lower Saxony shocked many observers by awarding Herbert Gruhl a highly prestigious state honor. "With his international best-seller *A Planet Is Plundered*," minister Monika Greifahn said, Gruhl has "placed ideas of environmental protection and care at the forefront of public political consciousness."[122]

A Social Ecology of Freedom

A combination of nationalism, authoritarianism, and yearnings for charismatic leaders that is legitimated by a mystical and biologistic "ecology" is potentially socially catastrophic. Just as the *völkisch* movement ultimately was channeled into the Nazi movement, so too new social movements that appeal to these concepts must be mindful of their potential for political and social catastrophe if they are channeled into a dangerous political direction that draws on mysticism.

A love of the natural world and alienation from modern society are in themselves innocent and legitimate ideas, and it was by no means a historical necessity that they be permutated into a justification for mass murder. Nor is "ecology" limited to an interpretation as a social Darwinist racial jungle, or politicized along tribal, regional, and nationalist lines. Nor is "ecology" inherently an antirational, mystical concept. Finally, the ecological crisis can hardly be dismissed; it is itself very real and is worsening rapidly. Indeed, the politicization of ecology is not only desirable but necessary.

Although this article has focused on the "ecological" right in the Federal Republic, "ecological" fascism is hardly limited to that country. In Britain, a wing of the National Front issues the cry, "Racial preservation is Green!" In the United States, the notorious white supremacist Tom Metzger remarks:

> I've noticed that there's an increased number of young people in the white racialist movement who are also quite interested in ecology, protecting the animals from cruelty and things like that, and it seems to me that as we are becoming more aware of our precarious state, the white man, the white woman's, state in the world, being only about 10 percent of the population, we begin to sympathize, empathize more, with the wolves and other animals.[123]

His colleague Monique Wolfing agrees: "Well, naturally. They're in the same position we are. Why would we want something created for ourselves and yet watch nature be destroyed? We work hand in hand with nature and we should save nature along with trying to save our race."[124] The noted U.S. deep ecologist Bill Devall, who is certainly not a fascist, has allowed anti-immigration themes to enter his views: He notes with apparent relief that while "population is beginning to stabilize in Western Europe and North America," there is a caveat—"in-migration." Devall chastises those who would "justify large-scale in-migration to Western Europe and North America from Latin America and Africa" as guilty of "misplaced humanism."[125]

What is clearly crucial is how an ecological politics is conceived. If the Green slogan "we are neither left nor right but up front" was ever meaningful, the emergence of an "ecological right" defines the slogan's bankruptcy conclusively. The need for an ecological left is urgent, especially one that is firmly committed to a clear, coherent set of anticapitalist, democratic, antihierarchical views. It must have firm roots in the internationalism of the left and the rational, humanistic, and genuinely egalitarian critique of social oppression that was part of the Enlightenment, particularly its revolutionary libertarian offshoot.

But an ecologically oriented politics must deal with biological phenomena warily, since interpretations of them can serve sinister ends. When "respect for Nature" comes to mean "reverence," it can mutate ecological politics into a religion that "Green Adolfs" can effectively use for authoritarian ends. When "Nature," in turn, becomes a metaphor legitimating sociobiology's "morality of the gene," the glories of "racial purity," "love of *Heimat*," "woman equals nature," or "Pleistocene consciousness," the cultural setting is created for reaction. "Ecological" fascism is a cynical but potentially politically effective attempt to mystically link genuine concern for present-day environmental problems with time-honored fears of the "outsider" or the "new," indeed the best elements of the Enlightenment, through ecological verbiage. Authoritarian mystifications need not be the fate of today's ecology movement, as social ecology demonstrates. But they could become its fate if ecomystics, ecoprimitivists, misanthropes, and antirationalists have their way."

Right-wing Ecology in Germany: Assessing the Historical Legacy

The original edition of *Ecofascism* appeared at a transitional moment, shortly after the Oklahoma City bombing brought right-wing extremism to broad public attention in North America. At a time when debates on the Unabomber agitated much of the radical milieu, there was relatively little literature in English on the subjects the book examined, and virtually none written for an activist rather than an academic audience. That has changed substantially in the intervening years. Today there are a variety of historical studies of the topic, and many people involved in ecological and social change movements have engaged critically with the challenges this history poses for our own time. The initial impetus for the book arose from the experience of both authors in various green movements in the 1980s and 1990s. We noticed that a number of prominent themes in contemporary environmentalist politics bore an unnerving resemblance to ideas put forward by reactionary movements and far-right figures, both historically and in the waning years of the twentieth century. Our aim was to provide critical perspective on the legacy of reactionary ecology in order to support and encourage a radical and emancipatory ecology. This remains my aim today. If ecological activists are unaware of the political trajectory these concepts have taken in the past, we will be unprepared for the next shift in the ideological terrain.

The book had a widely varying reception and was published in Norwegian, Greek, Czech, and several other languages. Its arguments were taken up and extended by a variety of authors in the years following the original publication.[1] While historians at first took little evident notice of it, particularly perceptive early reviews came from feminist philosopher Claudia Card and anarchist scholar Ronald Creagh.[2] Some conservative readers, meanwhile, greeted the book as confirmation of their own hostility toward environmentalism, fundamentally misunderstanding the issues at stake. Indeed on several revealing occasions, right-wing politicians and pundits attempted to enlist the book in campaigns to discredit ecological politics as a whole. In one noteworthy instance in 2003, the book achieved temporary notoriety in Australia when senator George Brandis read extensive excerpts from *Ecofascism* to a parliamentary session as part of an attack on the Australian Greens, likening them to Nazis. When Australian journalists contacted me for comment, I took the opportunity to clarify both the historical context and the contemporary relevance of ecology's problematic past.[3] Since the Brandis episode encapsulates many common misconstruals of the book's argument, I reproduce my response here:

Greens and Nazis

Historians rarely enjoy their fifteen minutes of fame, particularly when their work covers an obscure topic. Even if somebody out there ends up reading what we write, as likely as not we'll complain that they've missed the point. When you're thoroughly immersed in a subject, it can be hard to convey the nuances and complexities involved in a way that makes sense to a broad audience.

So it's probably not too surprising that I was less than thrilled to find my work at the center of a political controversy in faraway Australia, a place I have never visited and know little about. When Senator Brandis took the floor of the parliament and quoted at length from a book that I co-authored, he used my writing for purposes that are quite at odds with my own. There is nothing wrong with that in principle; it isn't my job to tell others what lessons they ought to draw from the events and movements I study. In this case, however, I think it important to point out that my scholarship offers little support for the conclusions Senator Brandis reached.

He is not the only reader of my work to draw such conclusions. I have heard from a number of conservative political figures in the United States, where I live, who are eager to use my historical work as a weapon in the struggle against what they see as the Green menace. These people refer to my research on ecofascism as a cheap tactic to impugn virtually all varieties of political environmentalism. In my opinion, this is not a serious way to approach important historical questions.

The book that caught Senator Brandis's attention is titled *Ecofascism: Lessons from the German Experience.* Along with my co-author Janet Biehl, I explore there the little-known legacy of right-wing ecology and its appropriation by one faction of the Nazi party in the 1930's. Our book says quite explicitly that there is no inherent connection between classical fascism and contemporary Green politics. What gave rise to the convergence of ecology and fascism seventy years ago was a specific set of historical circumstances and a specific version of ecological thinking, which our book examines in detail.

The excerpts which Senator Brandis presented to his colleagues ignored this crucial context, and thus failed to do justice both to the very grave history that the book recounts, as well as to the current relevance of these issues in today's world. Moreover, the concrete parallels that Brandis emphasized – an ostensible excess of radical zeal on the part of some Australian Greens, as well as their supposedly cynical attitude toward democratic institutions – are at best tangentially related to the ideological commonalities between environmentalism and fascism that my research reveals. The Nazis certainly did not come to power because the predecessors of the Greens in Germany were too vocal in their opposition to the militarist and authoritarian tendencies of their day.

It is possible that the Australian Greens are indeed awash in mystical and antihumanist ideas, as Senator Brandis's portrait would have it; to comment on that question exceeds my competence. If such is the case, however, it scarcely means that fascism is on its way. Perhaps Brandis's ill-considered invocation of the rise of Nazism will have a salutary effect after all, if it spurs his intended targets among the Greens to study this background further. For the present, however, it would seem that vociferous disagreement with the status quo – even if its tenor is too strident for some – represents a significant bulwark against political demagoguery, not a step toward dictatorship. That Senator Brandis apparently confused this sort of vigorous dissent with the lack of dissent that allowed fascism to flourish in the first place indicates that we still have a lot to learn from the history of political shortsightedness.

Such explanations are of limited effectiveness against organized demagogy, but they are essential to comprehending why *Ecofascism* was originally published and why it remains relevant today. Misunderstandings of the book were not, of course, confined to the right. A number of ecologically-oriented readers, whether liberals or leftists or anarchists, objected to it for the same reasons that garnered misplaced approval on the right. Deep ecologists were unsurprisingly displeased with the book, complaining that the very notion of an ecofascist politics was illusory and merely an "attack term" without historical or contemporary significance.[4] Liberal environmentalists and neo-pagans were similarly irritated by our analysis, believing that we had posited a "causal link" between environmentalism and fascism.[5] Other critical reactions were less naïve, such as the detailed assessment by David Watson of the *Fifth Estate*, and the book may even have played a role in instigating a process of clarification within the anarcho-primitivist milieu.[6] Even here the misunderstandings were sometimes remarkable; Watson, for example, surmised that I oppose organic farming as potentially fascist. My actual position is just the contrary: I want a vibrant and politically conscious organic farming movement, and that means coming to terms with the less pleasant aspects of the movement's past.

In addition to direct responses such as these, *Ecofascism*'s core themes have received thoughtful attention from a range of viewpoints. Deep ecologist Michael Zimmerman has published a series of discerning articles on ecofascism which make particularly salutary reading for those uncomfortable with a social ecology perspective.[7] A number of mainstream accounts have offered important historical insights while placing German traditions of reactionary ecology into broader context.[8] More indiscriminate treatments of the topic have tended to reduce the legacy of ecofascism to a simplistic tale meant to expose the dangers of any radical ecological engagement.[9] The religious aspects of far-right ecological thought have also generated significant scholarship.[10] This record of detailed research offers important historical background which can serve to refute two equally absurd claims: that "environmentalism is fascism" and that there are no connections whatsoever between environmentalism and fascism.

From the Past to the Present

Beyond historical matters, the persistence of ecofascist tendencies in contemporary politics and culture remains an important concern. Peter Zegers has provided an incisive overview of the ongoing legacy of reactionary ecology, while others have analyzed the continuing role of ecofascist ideas and groups in Britain, North America, and elsewhere.[11] In some cases these tendencies do not take an openly fascist form but bring together reactionary ecological themes with anti-immigrant sentiment, eugenic policies, and a nationally or racially tinged defense of the land. Prominent examples include the Finnish deep ecologist Pentti Linkola, among others. Both the Danish People's Party and the British National Party combine anti-immigrant politics with right-wing environmentalism, while the 'New Right' in both Germany and France champions ecology and bioregionalism. On the Italian far right, comparable strands can be found around the groups Forza Nuova and Alternativa Sociale. Similar tendencies are not difficult to discern in North American environmentalism, where ostensibly ecological justifications for opposing immigration are all too common, in some cases affiliated with repellent racial ideologies, and where figures like Garrett Hardin or John Tanton have little trouble attracting followers and supporters.[12] The struggles over population control and immigration policy within the Sierra Club in 1998 and again in 2004 are recent reflections of such strands, but they have a lengthy history within the US conservation movement.[13]

In the post-1945 German context, the subject of Janet Biehl's chapter, these developments have a more powerful resonance, and an extensive critical literature on the topic has emerged since *Ecofascism* was initially published. In particular, Jonathan Olsen's book *Nature and Nationalism* and Oliver Geden's book *Rechte Ökologie* provide abundant detail on the politics of right-wing ecology in Germany, amply confirming and extending Biehl's analysis.[14] Indeed the post-war connections between environmentalism and far-right politics have been studied in considerable depth in Germany, yielding a substantial body of work that deserves more attention than it generally receives among ecologically inclined readers.[15] At the same time, it would be a mistake to conclude that this is a peculiarly German phenomenon; recent research has revealed a long history of similar trends in British political culture, among others.[16] For those concerned about the political direction of the ecological movement, the legacy of figures like Rolf Gardiner and Jorian Jenks merits critical consideration.

One theme that figured less prominently in *Ecofascism* bears further analysis: the predilection of some forms of alternative spirituality toward reactionary ecology. Two of the more troubling examples are certain strands of neo-paganism and the anthroposophical movement founded by Rudolf Steiner. Many contemporary anthroposophists and neo-pagans appear entirely unaware of the historical entwinement of their movements with deeply regressive political tendencies and are consequently taken aback when confronted with this unexamined history. Indeed some readers mistook the book for a thinly veiled attack on neo-paganism as a whole or on anthroposophy as a whole, depending on their personal affiliations, and dismissed the evidence assembled here as the fruit of mean-spirited sectarianism or of hostility to spirituality as such. These are perilously naïve responses. There is an extensive historical literature examining the politics of both neo-paganism and anthroposophy, along with other forms of esoteric and New Age spirituality, much of which explores their affinities with reactionary ecological ideas.[17] Ignoring or denying these affinities does nothing to reduce their potency.

Esoteric and pagan worldviews are perennially popular not only within alternative spiritual circles and environmental movements but on the far right as well. As one example among many, here is an excerpt from the 2000 political position statement of the Pagan Liberation League, a white supremacist group in the Pacific Northwest:

> The PLL stands opposed to all forms of capitalist exploitation of the environment and we view any attack or intrusion upon Mother Nature as a personal attack against ourselves. We will fight the Corporate State to the death to preserve the natural beauty of the earth and its species and various races, most prominently our own species, the Aryan Species. We acknowledge that it has been chiefly the Aryan Species that has been at the forefront of the Environmental 'Green' movement, from the beginning, despite the fact that many of the pseudo-ecology organizations today who are finance-motivated betray the Aryan Spirit. We acknowledge that the true Green movement had its most radical, militant and holistic germination during the Third Reich and hereby declare ourselves to be in a Spiritual War with what we call the Judeo-Capitalist Status Quo.

The Pagan Liberation League statement continues:

> Blood and Soil, Back to the Land, and Homesteading: We
> advocate that our Folk learn how to live self-sufficiently, as
> free and independent of the System as is realistically possible.
> Studying animal husbandry, organic farming and herbal
> medicine are the ways of the future.[18]

Comparable passages can be found in far-right celebrations of anthroposophy.[19] The conflation of left and right positions in such statements represents a prominent tendency in contemporary culture and is another reason why the legacy of ecofascism warrants sustained attention among those working for an emancipatory ecological politics. For some, of course, the very notion of distinguishing right from left is futile. This stance reflects a widespread historical and political confusion which impedes meaningful debate and analysis. As Janet Biehl notes in her chapter, the foolish slogan "neither left nor right" was introduced into green politics by the right-wing authoritarian Herbert Gruhl. But the roots of the neither-left-nor-right idea go considerably further back; a version of this standpoint was popular within the nationalist and populist *völkisch* movement in Wilhelmine and Weimar Germany, and the pretence of offering a 'third way' between left and right was a central component in the rise of classical European fascism. Neo-fascist groups have continued this trend, attempting to recruit leftist youth via appeals to ecological themes as 'beyond left and right.'[20]

Though not as pronounced as its German counterpart, Italian Fascism also contained environmentalist impulses, another historical example—however ambivalent—of ecofascism in practice.[21] From land reclamation and ruralization projects to reforestation efforts, such impulses played a subordinate but noticeable role in Mussolini's Italy, often enough tied to racial and national ideology. In his 1921 article "Fascism and the Land" Mussolini declared that Fascism's goal was "to reclaim the land, and with the land the men, and with the men the race."[22] The 'land improvement' campaign launched in 1928 included measures to reduce urban sprawl, discourage monocropping in agriculture, protect the soil and promote non-mechanized methods of cultivation. By the 1930s exponents of the campaign announced that in Fascist Italy "we are witnessing a return to Mother Earth."[23] The president of the Fascist Agricultural Association for the province of Trent, Luciano Chimelli, was an ardent proponent of organic farming. According to Chimelli, "the climate created by Fascism" was especially hospitable to organic agriculture.[24] In 1940 the chief German organic farming journal extolled Fascism for rescuing the Italian landscape, for "saving the soil and thereby saving the race."[25] Admirers of Fascism's ecological orientation celebrated the reforestation programs in particular, declaring that these environmental achievements were only possible under the Fascist regime.

Ecofascism Re-examined

Despite this variegated and complex history, most of the public interest in fascist ecology has gravitated toward the singular case of Nazi Germany, whose unparalleled destructiveness seems so crassly at odds with any form of environmental concern. This was the subject of my chapter, and it remains an ongoing part of my historical research. The original chapter contained several errors, some relatively minor and some closer to the core of my argument. Since we have chosen to republish the text unrevised, I would like to correct these errors here. The claim that Ernst Haeckel joined the Thule Society late in his life, which I adopted from Daniel Gasman's work, appears to be groundless.[26] The claim that the Nazis created the first nature preserves in Europe is also mistaken. The statistic I provided from Raymond Dominick's work, that 60 percent of Weimar-era conservationists joined the Nazi party before 1939, refers not to the entire membership of conservationist organizations but to the leadership stratum. I characterized Rudolf Hess as a committed follower of Rudolf Steiner; in light of Hess's nebulous occult inclinations, I now think that description was mistaken.[27] Beyond details such as these, my figure of tens of thousands of farms encompassed by the organic farming campaign is much too high; the actual figure is probably closer to two thousand. Last, my brief depiction of the politics of Monism was one-sided. A fuller portrait of "the politically highly ambivalent Monist movement" shows that Monism, "oscillating between middle-class left social reform and *völkisch* ideals of the New Right," never achieved a clear or coherent political profile.[28]

Since the original edition of *Ecofascism* appeared, these subjects have received extensive additional study from historians in Germany and in the English-speaking world, particularly in the past decade, and this research has added considerably to our detailed knowledge of the topic.[29] In several cases these historians have presented perfunctory but significant criticisms of my argument.[30] While there are continuing debates on important aspects of the topic, and while I disagree with central components of the recent revisionist approach, I consider a number of these criticisms legitimate. Subsequent treatments have properly offered a more nuanced and complex account than the one I provided; scholarly analyses are not the same as straightforwardly political arguments for an activist audience, and my essay on the 'green wing' of the Nazis was not directed primarily at my colleagues in the historical profession but at my comrades in the ecological movement. My hope is that ecological activists will take the opportunity to learn from the debates among historians. Toward that end, I would like to survey some of the ongoing historical disagreements on environmental politics in the Nazi era.

A crucial point of dispute concerns the relation between environmental tendencies before 1933 and their appropriation under the Nazis. My argument highlighted ideological continuities extending from nineteenth-century Romanticism and figures like Arndt and Riehl through the Youth Movement of the Wilhelmine and Weimar eras, but the same ideological legacy can be traced via early twentieth-century nature protection organizations and the landscape preservation movement.[31] Some of the recent scholarship challenges this claim, arguing that a "great difference" divides Nazi forms of naturism from the movements that preceded them.[32] In some cases this line of reasoning culminates in the re-assuring insistence that "idealistic" and "naïve" approaches to "turning toward nature" were "far removed from romantic and racist ones."[33] Comforting as this notion may be, as a historical claim it is unfortunately false. In reality, many naïve and idealistic forms of turning toward nature found themselves in conspicuous proximity to romantic and racist forms, and still do today. Making sense of both past and present requires taking that historical proximity seriously.

As another historian has observed, summarizing the purportedly re-assuring line of argument, "the fact that the Nazis co-opted conservation does not mean that conservationists were proto-Nazis."[34] This is certainly true, but misses the point. Of course German conservationists were not all proto-Nazis, though some of them were. The problem is that pre-Nazi conservationism provided fertile ground for proto-Nazi ideas and practices, making the eventual process of co-optation all the easier. The same is true for a range of other movements that shared considerable overlap with early environmentalism, particularly the disparate *Lebensreform* or lifestyle reform tendencies, including vegetarianism, animal rights, natural healing, and back to the land movements. Much of the recent literature on these tendencies attempts to rehabilitate them by emphasizing their distance from later Nazi manifestations.[35] A more perspicacious approach would be to refine and clarify the moments of continuity and discontinuity in an effort to discern which implicit or explicit political and ideological dispositions lent themselves to appropriation by various strands of Nazism. The connections linking *Lebensreform* ideals with the *völkisch* milieu, for example, were substantial and wide-ranging, and an array of Nazi officials worked to incorporate *Lebensreform* principles and practices into the National Socialist state.[3]

Lineages of Right-Wing Ecology

Another point of contention concerns individual figures such as Ernst Haeckel and Martin Heidegger, both of whom have vocal defenders as well as detractors. Many of the debates surrounding these thinkers are only tangentially related to their role in the development of right-wing ecology, but are historically instructive nonetheless. Even Heidegger's admirers have largely come to acknowledge that he was an active Nazi, though disputes continue over the significance of this fact for understanding his philosophical works.[37] The more relevant question in the present context is the relation of Heidegger's thought to other right-wing perspectives preoccupied with similar themes of 'rootedness in the soil' and 'authenticity' and the baleful effects of modern technology.[38] In the case of Haeckel, the politics of ecology have been overshadowed by the politics of evolution, as scrutiny of his contested legacy has become embroiled in debates with intellectually threadbare variants of contemporary creationism. Oddly, the advocates of severely misguided 'intelligent design' ideology have sometimes been more realistic in their assessment of Haeckel's racial views than the defenders of Darwinism.[39] Daniel Gasman's work on Haeckel, meanwhile, has been subjected to rigorous criticism, much of it justified.[40] His focus on the underside of Haeckel's Social Darwinism nonetheless remains in many ways appropriate and necessary. The historical stature of Haeckel and Heidegger is not in dispute; what bears further examination is the influence of certain strands in their work on reactionary varieties of ecological thought.

That Haeckel coined the term 'ecology' and left a sizeable imprint on early popularization of ecological ideas does not in itself mean that ecology is inextricable from his political views. What it means is that the political history of ecological thinking is more complicated and ambivalent than we might wish. Simplistic versions of the 'from Haeckel to Hitler' argument are obviously untenable, but this scarcely alleviates the fundamental problem of Haeckel's combination of Social Darwinism, eugenics, theories of racial superiority and German nationalism. The point is not to posit one single all-explaining overarching narrative of how Germany got to 1933, but to take account of the specific strands that eventually contributed to the environmental aspects of National Socialism and are most relevant to comprehending the legacy of right-wing ecology. That project requires paying attention to the ideas at stake as well as to the structural factors and institutional frameworks which allowed such ideas to be put into practice; it includes tracing both longer-term cultural and ideological trends and the crucial shifts and dislocations brought about by World War I.[41] While the ecological components of Nazism may seem incidental to the overall historical narrative of the rise of National Socialism, they are not incidental to the history of ecological politics.

The status of environmental tendencies in Nazi Germany is of course contested among historians, and was indeed contested at the time, with powerful factions in party and state opposing the efforts of the 'green wing' from the beginning of Hitler's dictatorship. The resulting intra-Nazi struggles left a conflicted and complex record. Some scholars avoid this complexity by denying that there was any green wing within the Nazi movement.[42] Such a position simply ignores the evidence examined in this book. The notion of a 'green wing,' which I borrowed from Jost Hermand's work,[43] is not meant to suggest an identifiably coherent faction within the party or a smoothly cooperating group of fully like-minded cadre – several of its leading representatives were in fact consistently at odds with one another. Rather the term refers to a tendency or shared ideological and practical orientation, common to a number of activists and officials in the Nazi movement and regime, the main outlines of which are recognizably environmentalist by today's standards. As Robert Proctor has noted, "fascist ideals fostered research directions and lifestyle fashions that look strikingly like those we today might embrace."[44] This constellation of green trends can be construed narrowly or broadly; on a broad interpretation it might include proclivities toward animal rights, vegetarianism, natural nutrition and whole foods, and natural methods of health care, for example, each of which garnered significant support from various segments of the Nazi apparatus.[45] A narrower interpretation of Nazi environmentalism would focus instead on core features such as nature protection projects, ecologically oriented landscape planning, and organic agriculture.

Fascist Ecology in Practice

An especially forthright figure in promoting nature preservation and landscape protection under National

Socialist auspices was Alwin Seifert, who has been described as "the most prominent environmentalist in the Third Reich."[46] Among other activities, Seifert designed the biodynamic garden at Rudolf Hess's villa, but his pre-eminent contribution was supervising environmental standards on major building projects, most famously the construction of the Autobahn system, which was overseen by a coterie of "advocates for the landscape" under Seifert's direction. Their task was to preserve wetlands and environmentally sensitive areas of the countryside as much as possible, to ensure that large public works projects were ecologically sustainable, and to embed the new Autobahn roadways harmoniously into the surrounding landscape.[47] Seifert and his colleagues were not merely defensively 'greening' a concrete behemoth. The new highways traversed areas that had been thoroughly domesticated for centuries; there was no question of destroying wilderness. Despite their administratively weak position, Seifert's landscape advocates pro-actively used the project to nurture ecological diversity and rollback monoculture.

Like a number of other Nazi environmentalists, Seifert enjoyed an influential role in the post-war conservation movement, and after 1945 he strongly downplayed his activities and convictions during the Third Reich. Seifert joined the Nazi party in 1938, but during his post-war de-Nazification hearings claimed falsely that he had been made a party member without his knowledge and against his will.[48] In reality, Seifert made full use of his Nazi credentials until the bitter end of Hitler's regime, continuing his friendly correspondence with other Nazi officials into 1945, and just a year before the collapse of Nazi Germany he was promoted to the rank of General within the *Organisation Todt*.[49] He was involved in *völkisch* organizations well before 1933 and published extensively in Nazi periodicals, celebrating the environmental achievements of National Socialism.[50] It is these sorts of continuities spanning the pre-Nazi and post-Nazi periods that are of historical importance in understanding the continuing relevance of right-wing ecology, despite the modest degree of Seifert's actual accomplishments under Hitler's dictatorship. In several respects Seifert represents the very embodiment of an ecofascist outlook: he belonged to the *Wandervogel* movement as a young man, combined antisemitic views with mystical spiritual inclinations, and was influenced by various abstruse racial mythologies; he was a vociferous champion of organic agriculture in the Third Reich; and he became a principal figure in shaping Nazi environmental policy, putting his ideas into practice with the help of prominent Nazi leaders, from Todt and Hess to Himmler and Darré.

As important as Seifert is to understanding the ecological facets of Nazism, and as difficult as his relations may have been with other Nazi officials, he was hardly an isolated individual. Several of his 'advocates for the landscape' were supporters of biodynamic cultivation, including Max Karl Schwarz, "a dedicated proponent of National Socialist blood and soil ideology."[51] Schwarz, an anthroposophist and important leader in the biodynamic movement, introduced Seifert to biodynamic principles and was responsible for applying biodynamic methods to the Autobahn project.[52] Nazi conservationists like Walther Schoenichen, mentioned only briefly in my chapter, represented a similar hybrid of ecology and fascism. The same is true even for some of Seifert's rivals, such as Hans Schwenkel or Heinrich Wiepking-Jürgensmann, who played a significant part in the attempt to shape Nazi policy in the conquered territories of Eastern Europe along environmental lines.[53] The development of German forestry during the Nazi era provides yet another instance of environmentalist trends under National Socialist sponsorship.[54] The extent and variety of such examples suggests that the phenomenon of ecological participation in the Nazi regime was not a peripheral or passing matter.

Organic Agriculture under Nazi Patronage

Perhaps the most contentious theme in the existing scholarship on 'green' facets of Nazism is the status of organic farming.[55] The controversial nature of this topic reflects the vexed relationship between Nazism's 'blood and soil' ideals and the concrete realities of ecological practice. Historically informed study of the question has been hampered for several decades by the work of British researcher Anna Bramwell, whose conspicuously sympathetic portrayal of Richard Walther Darré cast him as leader of a group of "Green Nazis." Bramwell's extended apologia for the Nazi race theorist and Minister of Agriculture emphasized his support for biodynamic agriculture, the anthroposophical version of organic farming. Her works contain much valuable information, but her interpretations are consistently distorted and have been rightly challenged by a range of scholars.[56] Bramwell's efforts to condone Darré's racial views, for example, or her risible depiction of Darré as an anti-imperialist, stand in stark contrast to standard historical accounts, which recognize Darré as "the main theoretician of eastward continental expansion and agricultural settlement."[57] Many of Bramwell's concrete claims have also been disproven.[58]

In some cases, however, the fully justified critiques of Bramwell's work have overcompensated for her errors and produced a mirror image of her idealized portrait of Darré's enthusiasm for organic farming, thus yielding an opposite but similarly deficient image of the complex historical reality. Several of Bramwell's critics have overemphasized Darré's skepticism toward anthroposophy while neglecting the crucial support for biodynamics provided by Darré's staff. The reaction against Bramwell has even led some historians to deny that Darré supported organic farming at all.[59] This is a serious error. It is true that the biodynamic movement failed to obtain the coveted support of the Nazi agriculture minister and patron of 'blood and soil' ideology for most of the 1930s; although biodynamic principles converged with several of his core ideals, such as pastoral romanticism paired with hostility toward materialism, a return to an agrarian social order, and the vision of a simpler and healthier rural life, Darré was initially doubtful toward biodynamic farming and its anthroposophical underpinnings.[60] He looked askance at organic claims of higher quality produce and increased soil fertility and was decidedly unsympathetic to biodynamic efforts to curry favor within the network of agricultural institutions he oversaw. Darré also feuded with Seifert in 1936 and 1937, further distancing him from the biodynamic movement.

But his attitude began to shift in early 1939, due in part to economic exigencies and in part to the persistent work of the pro-biodynamic faction among the higher-level personnel around Darré, including anthroposophist members of his staff.[61] In January 1939 biodynamic advocates initiated a concerted campign to convince Rosenberg, Göring, Himmler and other party leaders that organic agriculture offered the path toward the future for Nazi Germany.[62] Darré's perspective now changed markedly. Reversing his earlier stance, Darré announced in January 1940 that biodynamic cultivation potentially constituted an equal partner with conventional farming in "maintaining and enhancing the productive capacity of the German soil."[63] The following year he declared that biodynamic farming was the only route to "the biological salvation of Europe."[64] Though still distrusting its anthroposophical origins, from 1940 onward Darré attempted to provide concrete support for biodynamic producers and to make organic food an integral part of Germany's wartime economy. As his institutional power dwindled and his own position became more precarious, he went to elaborate lengths to circumvent anti-biodynamic officials in the agriculture ministry and the Reich Food Estate, above all his subordinate and rival Herbert Backe, who eventually replaced him in 1942.[65] At times Darré made official statements distancing himself and his staff from biodynamic methods, even while working behind the scenes to advance them.[66]

During his last two years of nominal control of the agricultural apparatus, Darré and the biodynamic supporters on his staff vigorously promoted organic farming through a series of semi-private associations, with personnel chosen for their loyalty to Darré and their sympathy for biodynamics.[67] These included staff members in the office of the Reich

Peasant Leader and the Nazi party's Office of Agrarian Policy who were committed to biodynamic agriculture. Darré adopted the phrase 'farming according to the laws of life' as a euphemism for the biodynamic version of organic agriculture; the terms were often used interchangeably. The measures showed some success for a time; in June 1941 Darré noted with satisfaction that "several circles in the highest leadership of the NSDAP have come to endorse biodynamic agriculture."[68] Some Nazi supporters of biodynamic methods were undoubtedly motivated by war-related concerns over the availability of raw materials rather than by any interest in ecological sustainability, and Darré's plans for large-scale sponsorship of biodynamic farming eventually came to naught as his effective influence waned. The meager practical outcome of such endeavors does not mean that Darré was insufficiently committed to organic farming; instead it indicates that even the concerted efforts of a Reich Minister who had fallen out of official favor were of little use in the face of opposition from other Nazi agricultural authorities.

The Politics of Blood and Soil

The peasant romanticism at the heart of Darré's worldview was not an anomaly in the Nazi milieu; Gottfried Feder's critique of urbanism or Otto Strasser's rural nostalgia display comparable tendencies.[69] Such beliefs were not, moreover, restricted to high-level officials like Darré or ideologues like Strasser. This ensemble of themes – the Nazi revival of ruralism, pastoral ideals, organicism, mythology of the peasantry, calls to return to the soil and become closer to the land for the good of the

Volk – extended to the lowest and most far-flung levels of the National Socialist apparatus.[70] Some scholars have argued that Darré had no interest whatsoever in organic farming during his tenure as Nazi minister, and that this notion was concocted by his defense attorneys at his post-war trial in Nuremberg. This interpretation is a significant misunderstanding. Darré's lawyer at Nuremberg was anthroposophist Hans Merkel, a specialist in agrarian law who had been a prominent member of Darré's staff since 1934. Along with his colleagues Hermann Reischle and Georg Halbe, Merkel was instrumental in changing Darré's stance toward biodynamic agriculture in the late 1930s. At Darré's Nuremberg trial, Merkel did portray the former Reich Minister as an idealistic protector of a revitalized peasantry as a supposedly mitigating factor, but the documentary record of Darré's active intervention on behalf of biodynamic agriculture during the Nazi era was by no means a post-war invention.

Merkel's own career is an exemplary instance of the longstanding intertwinement of biodynamic aspirations and Nazi institutional activities. He was initially recruited by Darré's assistant Hermann Reischle, an SS officer who had worked on the NSDAP's rural campaigns before Hitler came to power and who subsequently coordinated the pro-biodynamic grouping of Nazi agricultural functionaries from his position in the Reich Office for Agrarian Policy.[71] Merkel supervised the personnel who worked most closely with the Reich Peasant Leader.[72] He published widely on farming policy and wrote regularly for Darré's blood and soil journal *Odal*, combining organic metaphors with calls for expanded German *Lebensraum*.[73] Merkel had been a member of the Anthroposophical Society since 1926 and was both a faithful spokesman for Darré's ideas and a primary proponent of biodynamic cultivation within the Nazi agricultural apparatus. He continued to work with Darré and other veterans of the Nazi agrarian bureaucracy in promoting organic farming after 1945.[74] Darré, for his part, spent his time in prison studying Steiner's writings and maintained very friendly relations with anthroposophists and biodynamic advocates until his death in 1953.

Merkel was hardly alone among Darré's deputies. Georg Halbe was another anthroposophist who worked for Darré from 1935 to 1942, concentrating on publishing projects. He was a staff member at *Odal* and manager of the *Blut und Boden Verlag*, the Blood and Soil publishing house. One of his chief tasks as an employee of the Reich Food Estate was promoting organic farming in its biodynamic form.[75] Halbe wrote dozens of articles for Nazi publications, including essays on biodynamic agriculture, and in 1942 planned to publish a book on organic farming.[76] His writings combined agrarian romanticism, Germanic myths, antisemitism, a fondness for holism, and an emphatic commitment to National Socialism.[77] When Darré was replaced by Backe in 1942, Halbe left the agricultural apparatus and moved to the Ministry for the Occupied Eastern Territories, then in 1944 to the Propaganda Ministry. While Halbe worked largely behind the scenes, biodynamic practices were praised in print by prominent representatives of Nazi agriculture policy such as Hermann Schneider, a Reichstag member, SS colonel, and former 'Reich Inspector for the Battle of Production,' the Nazi program for agricultural autarky.[78] In 1939 Schneider visited the premier biodynamic estate in

Germany as Darré's representative, and in 1940 acclaimed biodynamics as the key to achieving natural nutrition and healthy soil and restoring the peasantry as the lifeblood of the nation.[79] Even staff members of the Wehrmacht high command supported biodynamics.[80] Whatever their effectiveness may have been, the actions of Nazi authorities on behalf of biodynamic cultivation point to another instance of partial synthesis between 'green' precepts and National Socialist ambitions.

In attempting to put such occurrences into historical context and refute the ex post facto apologias and obfuscations of figures like Bramwell and Merkel, recent scholarship has sometimes maintained that Darré and his companions genuinely cared only about 'blood' and not about 'soil,' were concerned solely with race, ruralism and rootedness and not with ecological considerations, and did not exhibit any authentic environmentalism. But the notion of a clear separation between environmental tendencies on the one hand and ruralism and racial ideology on the other hand is a post-1945 imposition, a projection of current values onto the past. From the Wilhelmine era through the Nazi period, these phenomena which now seem so obviously different were not consistently distinguished and were frequently combined in various amalgamations of rural romanticism, racial utopias, back-to-the-land ideals and proto-ecological sentiment. A view which "combined landscape aesthetics, ecological concern, and racial pride," notes David Blackbourn, "was shared by most conservationists."[81] Even today, of course, racist and ethnocentric assumptions have not somehow disappeared from environmental circles.

In the context of Nazism, the promotion of racial ideology and the promotion of organic agriculture went hand in hand all along, with biodynamic proponents serving in prominent positions in the racial bureaucracy as well.[82] Hermann Reischle was the founding head of the 'Race Bureau' in the SS Office of Race and Settlement, and much of his work focused on the racial advantages of rural re-settlement programs, bringing together the health of the nation and the health of the soil. He was also a major figure in planning the 'Germanization' of territories to be conquered in the East. Hans Merkel was another leading official in the SS Office of Race and Settlement (his title was *Führer beim Stab des Rasse- und Siedlungshauptamts*), the institutional embodiment of Nazi racialism and ruralism and of Darré's blood and soil doctrines. Albert Friehe, a Nazi politician and functionary of the biodynamic association, was a party expert on both agricultural policy and racial policy. In addition to promoting biodynamic farming, Friehe served simultaneously as a specialist for peasant concerns and a staff member of the NSDAP 'Office of Race Policy.'[83] By neglecting this imbrication of organic visions and racist structures, the historiographical debate over Nazi environmentalism has partly obscured the significance of the shift in official attitudes toward organic agriculture in the guise of biodynamics.

Biodynamic Farming and Nazism

If Darré was unconvinced of the virtues of organic farming until shortly before WWII began, the biodynamic movement had been eager to prove its National Socialist credentials for years, and had in fact cultivated contacts with Nazi circles well before Hitler's rise to power.[84] In 1933 the Reich League for Biodynamic Agriculture was founded under the leadership of anthroposophist Erhard Bartsch, with headquarters at Bartsch's estate in Bad Saarow. Biodynamic advocates touted their holistic version of organic agriculture as "spiritually aware peasant wisdom" in opposition to "civilization, technology, and modern urban culture."[85] Steiner's followers viewed Nazism's agrarian policy as a vindication of the biodynamic approach to farming and food, and despite opposition from the chemical industry, the agricultural establishment, and anti-occult sectors of the Nazi security apparatus, the biodynamic movement experienced impressive growth during the early years of the Third Reich.[86] Rather than a personal predilection of Darré or the peculiar preferences of Hess or the unpredictability of Himmler or the political promiscuity of biodynamics and its proponents, what the controversy over organic farming in Nazi Germany reveals is the ideological extent and practical significance of the overlap between ecological and National Socialist visions.

The biodynamic movement received extensive praise in the Nazi press, from the *Völkischer Beobachter* to rural venues and health periodicals.[87] Nazi supporters of biodynamics applauded Steiner's version of organic farming as a powerful weapon "in the National Socialist struggle against intellectualism and materialism, which are alien to our people."[88] Organic advocates returned the favor in *Demeter*, the biodynamic journal, emphasizing Nazism's effort to attain agricultural autarky for Germany.[89] A biodynamic dairy farmer from Silesia proclaimed in

1937 that both biodynamics and Nazism were based on "closeness to nature."[90] The front cover of the May 1939 issue of *Demeter* featured a bucolic picture of Adolf Hitler in an alpine landscape, surrounded by children, in honor of the Führer's fiftieth birthday. *Demeter* also celebrated Nazi Germany's military conquests and called for using prisoners of war in environmental projects.[91] Biodynamic publications combined anthroposophical, organic, and National Socialist vocabularies, including *Lebensraum* and blood and soil terminology, and touted the abundant contributions made by biodynamic practices to the environmental policy of the Third Reich.[92] Such ideological combinations carried a potent message; biodynamic representatives blamed profit-oriented chemical agriculture on the Jews, and their anti-materialist stance won them praise from Nazi antisemites.[93] Bartsch boasted with considerable justification that "the leading men of the Demeter movement have put themselves, their knowledge and experience wholeheartedly at the service of National Socialist Germany."[94]

A crucial source of institutional backing for the biodynamic movement came from Nazi *Lebensreform* officials, above all Hanns Georg Müller, a longtime Nazi who coordinated the various 'lifestyle reform' currents within the party.[95] From his post as an official in the *Reichsleitung*, the Nazi party directorate, Müller interceded repeatedly on behalf of biodynamic growers, backing them assertively in dealings with party organizations as well as private business associations. In 1938, for instance, he successfully intervened with the national potato producers guild to obtain favorable treatment for Demeter products.[96] Müller also published a series of biodynamic books and pamphlets in his publishing house and strongly promoted biodynamics in his journal *Leib und Leben.*[97] The journal was sponsored by the *Deutsche Gesellschaft für Lebensreform*, the official Nazi umbrella organization for 'lifestyle reform' groups, and took a zealous National Socialist line. Dozens of celebratory articles on biodynamics appeared in its pages, many of them written by senior officials in the Nazi *Lebensreform* movement. *Leib und Leben* and *Demeter* were sister journals and routinely advertised for one another. Among the prominent authors in *Leib und Leben* were biodynamic spokespeople, including Seifert and anthroposophist Franz Dreidax, who detailed the congruence of National Socialist ideals with biodynamic practices. Biodynamic growers were presented as pioneers of the natural German method of cultivation that had finally come into its own under the leadership of the Third Reich.[98]

Beyond aggressively publicizing its support for biodynamic agriculture, the Nazi *Lebensreform* apparatus welcomed the biodynamic movement as a leading force in its institutions. In 1935 the Reich League for Biodynamic Agriculture became a corporative member of the *Deutsche Gesellschaft für Lebensreform*, and Dreidax and Bartsch joined the organization's leadership council. The first principle of the association declared: "The worldview of the German *Lebensreform* movement is National Socialism."[99] Bartsch and Dreidax, the leading proponents of biodynamic farming in Germany, served for years as official representatives of the organization and promoted its combination of Nazi values and alternative cultural initiatives. With the energetic backing of Müller and his staff, biodynamic adherents publicly and actively symbolized Nazism's incorporation of environmentally oriented causes. The biodynamic movement also had ample opportunity to broadcast its views in the Nazi press.[100] Once the war began, Darré arranged to have Bartsch, Dreidax, and other biodynamic leaders exempted from military service.[101]

Alongside its institutional anchoring in Nazi Germany's *Lebensreform* organs, the Reich League for Biodynamic Agriculture added a remarkable array of Nazi luminaries to its roster of supporters. As early as April 1934 Nazi Interior Minister Wilhelm Frick visited Bartsch's biodynamic estate and expressed his encouragement for the organization. He was followed by a parade of similarly high-profile figures, including Hess, Darré, Rosenberg, Robert Ley, Otto Ohlendorf, Alfred Baeumler, and Rudi Peuckert, head of the Reich Office for Agricultural Policy and Nazi 'peasant leader' for Thuringia. These and other Nazi leaders explicitly voiced their support for biodynamic agriculture, while Bartsch and his colleagues gained notable sympathy and interest from the highest echelons of the party.[102] Above all, Hess and his lieutenants offered continual support for biodynamics throughout the 1930s. Demeter supplied the Rudolf Hess Hospital in Dresden with biodynamic products, and even Hitler's vegetable garden at Obersalzberg was farmed biodynamically.[103]

SS Adoption of Biodynamic Agriculture

Despite this conspicuous endorsement by a wide range of prominent Nazi officials, extending well beyond Darré and his staff, the biodynamic movement faced the combined resistance of opponents of organic farming within the agricultural apparatus and opponents of anthroposophy within the security services. SD and Gestapo agents considered biodynamic methods occultist quackery, a pointless encumbrance on traditional farming techniques. In their eyes, the biodynamic movement attempted "to spread the false international doctrine of anthroposophy disguised as National Socialism."[104] In June 1941, as part of the anti-occult campaign unleashed after Hess's flight to Britain, the Reich League for Biodynamic Agriculture was dissolved and Bartsch and other representatives of the movement were temporarily imprisoned, in spite of Darré's efforts to protect them. Remarkably, even this did not spell the end of biodynamic efforts in the Third Reich. The June 1941 actions removed Steiner's version of organic farming from public view, but scarcely eliminated it, as biodynamic initiatives continued apace under the unexpected protection of Himmler and the SS.

The cooperation between biodynamic growers and the SS had been underway for some time. Since the beginning of the war, biodynamic practitioners had been collaborating with the SS on various projects, including 'settlement' plans in the occupied East.[105] Biodynamic leaders saw the war as their chance to step forward in support of the German cause and as an auspicious occasion to re-shape Eastern lands along biodynamic lines. The Reich Food Estate recommended biodynamic cultivation for the annexed Eastern territories because it required no artificial fertilizers. As early as October 1939, the SS requisitioned a large farmstead in the occupied province of Posen to turn it into an agricultural training facility based on biodynamic principles, with the active cooperation of the Reich League for Biodynamic Agriculture.[106] Himmler's own attitude toward biodynamic farming was ambivalent; he rejected its anthroposophical foundations but appreciated its practical potential. After the June 1941 crackdown he ordered the agricultural sections of the SS to continue working with biodynamic methods, in cooperation with Bartsch, Dreidax, and their colleagues, but to keep these activities unobtrusive.[107] The term Himmler and his associates used to designate biodynamic agriculture was 'natural farming'.

Two of Himmler's most powerful lieutenants, Günther Pancke and Oswald Pohl, administered the SS biodynamic programs. Pancke was Darré's successor as head of the SS Office of Race and Settlement and played a leading role in the effort to alter conquered lands in the East according to Himmler's Germanic model once the racially 'unfit' inhabitants were forcibly removed. One of Pancke's goals was the establishment of agricultural estates in the Eastern territories governed by so-called 'soldier-farmers.' He considered biodynamic cultivation the suitable method for this would-be vanguard, pioneers of a racially dependable peasantry in the ethnically cleansed East, and the SS sent its personnel to attend courses provided by the Reich League for Biodynamic Agriculture.[108] Pancke's colleague Oswald Pohl was in charge of the economic enterprises of the SS and administrator of the concentration camp system. Pohl was a friend of Seifert and had his own estate farmed biodynamically. He sent Himmler biodynamic literature to demonstrate its value to the SS.[109] In January 1939 Himmler created a new SS corporation under

Pohl's supervision, the German Research Facility for Food and Nutrition, known by its German initials as the DVA. A substantial portion of its operations consisted of biodynamic plantations growing products for the SS and the German military, with production monitored by representatives of the Reich League for Biodynamic Agriculture. The biodynamic plantations were located at concentration camps, including Dachau and Ravensbrück, as well as estates in occupied Eastern Europe and in Germany. Ravensbrück was the first DVA estate to be converted to biodynamic cultivation, in May 1940. Eventually the majority of the DVA's plantations were run biodynamically.[110]

The DVA also marketed Demeter products, cooperated with Weleda, and contributed financially to the Reich League for Biodynamic Agriculture.[111] The head of the DVA's agricultural section was SS officer Heinrich Vogel, an outspoken proponent of biodynamics. The centerpiece of the DVA biodynamic operations was the sizeable plantation at Dachau, which produced medicinal herbs and other goods for the SS. As at Ravensbrück, the labor on the Dachau biodynamic plantation was performed by camp inmates. With the assistance of Vogel and Seifert, from 1941 onward the Dachau operation was overseen by anthroposophist SS officer Franz Lippert, a leader of the biodynamic movement from its beginnings and head gardener at Weleda from 1924 to 1940. In 1944 Lippert received special recognition and a bonus for his efforts at the Dachau plantation.[112] Lippert also published a book for the SS in 1942 based on his work at Weleda and Dachau.[113] Weleda additionally supplied biodynamic materials to SS doctor Sigmund Rascher, who performed infamous 'medical experiments' at Dachau involving the torture and death of many inmates. Rascher was an avid proponent of biodynamic methods, and in order to keep him supplied Weleda maintained ongoing business relationships with the SS and the Wehrmacht and was given special access to the SS's own stock of petroleum jelly, a rare commodity in war-time Germany.[114]

One of the tasks of the Dachau biodynamic plantation was to train 'settlers' for the Eastern territories, part of SS plans to use biodynamic cultivation in the environmental and ethnic re-ordering of the East.[115] Biodynamic leaders participated actively in these efforts, obtaining preferential treatment from the DVA and other SS agencies in return. In 1941, for example, the DVA offered members of the Reich League for Biodynamic Agriculture discount prices on their Dachau products.[116] In addition to figures like Bartsch, Seifert, and Schwarz, biodynamic representative Nicolaus Remer helped oversee agricultural production in the occupied Ukraine in 1941 and 1942, while Darré's ally Rudi Peuckert supplied forced labor from occupied lands for war-time agricultural production. In 1943 another leading biodynamic advocate, anthroposophist SS officer Carl Grund, was specially commissioned to assess biodynamic farming in the conquered Russian provinces.[117] Grund had been active in the biodynamic movement since the 1920s and was head of the 'Information Office for Biodynamic Agriculture.' On Himmler's orders, Grund was given a variety of special tasks and prerogatives as an expert for 'natural farming' in the East. Himmler also directed that former members of the Reich League for Biodynamic Agriculture be engaged in the re-organization of agriculture in the Eastern territories and thus contribute to the "practical work of reconstruction" being carried out by German forces.[118] SS sponsorship of biodynamics continued until the camps were liberated.

The Unsettling History of Nazi Ecology

Whether presented as "farming according to the laws of life" or as "natural farming" or as a trustworthy method for restoring the health and fertility of the German soil and the German people, biodynamic cultivation found numerous amenable partners in the Nazi hierarchy. It augured the return of a balanced relationship between the German nation and the German landscape, a regenerated community living in harmony with nature. Indeed the Third Reich can be seen as the time when biodynamic agriculture received its most significant levels of state support and achieved its most impressive status among high officials.[119] In historical perspective, the quotidian details of the biodynamic movement's intertwinement with Nazi environmental endeavors may be more illuminating than well-worn debates over the 'green' inclinations of Darré or other Nazi celebrities. Why, then, has there been such resistance to acknowledging these links?[120] In light of the extremely well documented degree of Nazi support for biodynamic agriculture, why do some historians, philosophers, political scientists and others continue to deny or downplay the topic's relevance?

Part of the difficulty has to do with a confusion between normative and descriptive claims. Focusing on what ecological thinking ought to be, some authors have overlooked what it actually has been historically.[121] This makes it harder rather than easier to discern which aspects of ecological thought are worth developing further. Another problem stems from the general challenges surrounding any effort to face the horrific legacy of National Socialism. Although the enormity of Nazism's crimes seems to render attempts to make historical sense of them futile, it is irresponsible to turn our eyes away from the subject. The close proximity – ideological as well as geographic – between Nazi programs for ecological renewal and Nazi programs for racial extermination suggests that further attention to this unlikely conjunction is called for. Boria Sax observes that "the Nazis murdered in the name of nature, invoking animals and landscapes."[122] Indeed "the National Socialist religion of nature," writes Robert Pois, "not only implicitly provided for extermination policies as a 'final solution', but in fact made them logically and, above all, *ethically* necessary."[123] The fact that war criminals like Ohlendorf and Pohl (both of whom were executed after the war for crimes against humanity) actively intervened on behalf of biodynamic agriculture lends further weight to this line of inquiry.

But the war and the holocaust were ecocidal as well as genocidal. Tracing the complex and contradictory history of Nazi naturism does not mean disregarding Nazism's enormously destructive impact on the European environment. It means taking seriously the countervailing proto-ecological tendencies within the Nazi regime, many of which sustained high levels of support from various sectors of the Nazi leadership for a remarkably long time and were notably successful on their own terms. These initiatives around environmentally sensitive public works, organic agriculture, habitat protection, and so forth were not mere camouflage or peculiar deviations from the destructive path of the Nazi juggernaut; they were part and parcel of the Nazi project for remaking the landscape of Europe, ethnically as well as ecologically. Ignoring their impact yields an impaired comprehension of the full dimensions of that project and its attempted implementation under the banner of blood and soil.

In other instances the implications of Nazi environmentalism do not seem to have been thought through, historically or philosophically or politically. One of the more astute recent historians of the topic has written: "Far from signaling a National Socialist commitment to nature preservation, highly publicized landscape protection measures, particularly the Imperial Nature Protection Law, were weak and ineffective."[124] This is a non-sequitur. Whether Nazi environmental measures actually worked, and whether they represented a National Socialist commitment to nature preservation, are not at all the same thing. It is one thing to argue that figures like Seifert did not really accomplish much and were sidelined by other Nazis, or that the alliances between Nazis and nature conservationists were merely tactical, and quite another thing to claim that this somehow vitiates the commitment to nature that some Nazis demonstrated or diminishes the significance of ecological themes in some varieties of Nazi thought or effaces the plentiful real-world partnerships that arose between environmentalists and Nazi officials. The considerable limitations of National Socialist environmental policy in practice do not by themselves negate the scope or substance of environmental endeavors in Nazi garb.

Similarly, an insistence on neater and more orderly ideological distinctions in this context can paradoxically obscure matters rather than illuminating them. For better or worse, the history of ideas is often much less tidy than we might prefer, and the conjoining of racial fantasies and rural idylls—which extended well beyond the confines of Nazi Germany—is not something that can be wished away by re-defining terms. Since the advent of industrial capitalism, for a number of commentators in Germany and elsewhere, the rise of urbanization seemed to go hand in hand with a loss of organic community and of a harmonious relationship with the natural landscape, and the return to rural simplicity promised to restore national or racial purity as well. Specious as such beliefs may have been, they exercised a powerful influence on several generations of thinkers.[125] The notion that enviromentalist enthusiasm for National Socialism was merely a matter of strategic appropriation of Nazi rhetoric fails to take account of the longstanding *völkisch* strands in early environmentalism and of green tendencies on the authoritarian right and their multivalent political and cultural reverberations, traditions which predated the rise of Nazism by decades. These ideas came to partial fruition under Hitler's regime, with Nazi environmental projects presented as a path to regenerating the nation and organic farming as a more natural diet for a heartier, healthier, and haler German people.

Making Sense of Right-wing Ecology Past and Present

The important historiographical differences involved in these debates cannot be definitively resolved here. But too many of the recent contributions to this ongoing debate are oriented toward debunking the notion that 'authentic' ecological elements played a significant role in the Nazi regime. I consider this approach a mistake. Much of Nazism based both its destructive and its 'constructive' aspects on a specifically naturalist vision, one that bore compelling and substantive parallels to ecological values, and these similarities were reflected in an expansive spectrum of institutions and practices. Minimizing Nazism's especially disturbing and unanticipated features does not relieve a burden for ecological activists today but conceals the continuities between some of the twentieth century's most cherished ideals and some of its most shameful crimes. Neglecting the 'green' features of Nazism is a deceptive way of shielding ourselves from what is most unsettling about the history of the topic.

To a certain extent, the strategy of deflecting this uncomfortable history has been led by liberal scholars who apparently mean to salvage the honor of environmentalism by disassociating it from the far right. From a radical perspective, this position is often based on political naïvete. Some historians seem to be defending the good name of German conservationists by pointing out that before 1933 they were apolitical liberals or mere conservatives, and just got pulled into the wake of the inexorably advancing Nazi juggernaut. Strangely, these analysts do not draw the lesson that an apolitical or liberal or conservative position was part of the problem in the first place, and that a radical ecologicial stance affiliated with a broader left politics might present a much more resistant alternative. Similar problems bedevil liberal interpretations of the fate of conservation once Hitler came to power. Summarizing a prominent line of argument in the recent literature, one historian writes that "even when conservationists ultimately succeeded, their victory had less to do with the popularity of the cause of nature protection than the chaotic interplay of actors, institutions and interests that characterised National Socialist governance. Often the most decisive factor was support from high-ranking Nazi officials whose motives were highly dubious."[126] How would that differ from environmental successes in latter-day capitalist democracies? The motives of Nazi officials who took an approving view of conservationist measures were no doubt 'highly dubious,' but so are the motives of liberal and conservative politicians, not to mention Green politicians, in many non-Nazi contexts. By the same token, dismissing figures like Hess and Darré merely as eccentric right-wingers who happened to be attracted to environmental thinking is not a historically serious way to comprehend the problem of reactionary ecology.[127] If we want to understand the appeal of National Socialism, it is essential to face such problems squarely.

In some cases, moreover, the desire to absolve early German conservationists by not associating them too closely with Nazism reflects not only a short-sighted perspective on the past but political timidity in the present. Grassroots ecological activists today do not shy away from criticizing Al Gore or Joschka Fischer; why shy away from criticizing the environmental establishment of yesteryear? The history of environmentalism consistently reveals an authoritarian and nationalist disposition in many disparate contexts, despite the efforts of some of our forebears to forge liberatory alternatives, and these factors are a legitimate object of critique, as are the bourgeois roots of much of mainstream conservationism and the colonial and imperialist roots of other ecological proposals and practices. A historical focus on the right-wing strands within ecological politics can help to clarify such matters and contribute to a more critical re-consideration of traditional environmental themes, from wilderness preservation to natural lifestyles to the basic relationship between humankind and the rest of the earth.[128] This sort of critical re-consideration is all the more important in an era when positions which seem radical and innovative do not in fact offer a meaningful challenge to the status quo.[129]

When historians play down the lengthy record of entwinement between ecological ideals and fascist realities, they reinforce a specific kind of historical naivete among ecological activists in the present, who then feel justified in ignoring this history rather than grappling with it head-on. When activists neglect to inform themselves about this contested history, they cede the field to Nazi nostalgists and purveyors of a putatively updated right-wing ecology. Those of us who reject nationalism and xenophobia and ideas of racial purity and oppose authoritarian solutions and reactionary panaceas have an obligation to be vocal about raising such issues in ecological contexts, as activists and as scholars. Otherwise we leave ourselves, our ideals, and our movements open to appropriation by right-wing forces hoping to recuperate fascist politics in 'alternative' attire. The ecological movement will be strengthened, not weakened, by coming to terms with the unacknowledged aspects of its past.

Exaggerated anxieties about guilt by association, understandable as they may be in the current context of anti-environmental backlash, are an inadequate response to the subject. There are indisputably critics of environmentalism ready to seize on any discussion of right-wing ecology in order to denounce green politics as such.[130] These concerns can be refuted by historically knowledgeable and politically decisive argument. The point of the research assembled in this book is not to induce guilt or shame but to instigate informed engagement with and conscious reflection on the underexamined aspects of our common inheritance. If greens today are 'guilty' of anything, it is historical ignorance, not Nazi sympathies. Avoidance will not address this challenge and will not avert attacks from those who consider environmental activism an elitist pastime and an imposition on personal liberties or community traditions. Rather than apologizing for our commitment to confronting the sources of ecological and social destruction, we can forthrightly claim an honorable legacy of radical green politics that acknowledges and abjures the mistakes of our predecessors. We do not honor our best aspirations by ignoring our past.

Part of purpose of this book is to raise such questions in spite of the discomfort they provoke. Definitive answers, on the other hand, are something that neither scholars nor activists can provide on our own; different readers will draw their own lessons from the history of ecofascism. It would be a welcome development if this history sparked a re-thinking of some of the political positions current within the contemporary environmental scene. Many of those positions are plainly inadequate in the face of the enduring social and ecological crisis. I remain a social ecologist fully committed to a thoroughgoing transformation of society and of human relations with the natural world. If ecological thinkers and activists do not foster lasting links to a broader left political practice and a comprehensive outlook based on radical social critique, we risk losing the creative potential, subversive possibilities, and challenging prospects of an approach which takes natural and social change equally seriously. Instead of historical indifference or discounting the compromises of our past, instead of capitulating to the apprehensions of the present, a clear-eyed assessment of this conflicted legacy can help us move toward a socially and ecologically hopeful future.

NOTES

FASCIST ECOLOGY: THE "GREEN WING" OF THE NAZI PARTY AND ITS HISTORICAL ANTECEDENTS
PETER STAUDENMAIER, 1995

1   Ernst Lehmann, *Biologischer Wille. Wege und Ziele biologischer Arbeit im neuen Reich,* München, 1934, pp. 10-11. Lehmann was a professor of botany who characterized National Socialism as "politically applied biology."

2   Anna Bramwell, author of the only book-length study on the subject, is exemplary in this respect. See her *Blood and Soil: Walther Darré and Hitler's 'Green Party',* Bourne End, 1985, and *Ecology in the 20th Century: A History,* New Haven, 1989.

3   See Raymond H. Dominick, *The Environmental Movement in Germany: Prophets and Pioneers, 1871-1971,* Bloomington, 1992, especially part three, "The Völkisch Temptation."

4   For example, Dominick, *The Environmental Movement in Germany,* , p. 22; and Jost Hermand, *Grüne Utopien in Deutschland: Zur Geschichte des ökologischen Bewußtseins*, Frankfurt, 1991, pp. 44-45.

5   Quoted in Rudolf Krügel, *Der Begriff des Volksgeistes in Ernst Moritz Arndts Geschichtsanschauung*, Langensalza, 1914, p. 18.

6   Wilhelm Heinrich Riehl, *Feld und Wald*, Stuttgart, 1857, p. 52.

7   Klaus Bergmann, *Agrarromantik und Großstadtfeindschaft*, Meisenheim, 1970, p. 38. There is no satisfactory English counterpart to "Großstadtfeindschaft," a term which signifies hostility to the cosmopolitanism, internationalism, and cultural tolerance of cities as such. This 'anti-urbanism' is the precise opposite of the careful critique of urbanization worked out by Murray Bookchin in *Urbanization Without Cities*, Montréal, 1992, and *The Limits of the City*, Montréal, 1986.

8   George Mosse, *The Crisis of German Ideology: Intellectual Origins of the Third Reich*, New York, 1964, p. 29.

9   Lucy Dawidowicz, *The War Against the Jews 1933-1945*, New York, 1975, pp. 61-62.

10 Daniel Gasman, *The Scientific Origins of National Socialism: Social Darwinism in Ernst Haeckel and the German Monist League*, New York, 1971, p. xvii.

11 ibid., p. 30. Gasman's thesis about the politics of Monism is hardly uncontroversial; the book's central argument, however, is sound.

12 Quoted in Gasman, *The Scientific Origins of National Socialism*, p. 34.

13 ibid., p. 33.

14 See the foreword to the 1982 reprint of his 1923 book *Die Entdeckung der Heimat*, published by the far-right MUT Verlag.

15 Mosse, *The Crisis of German Ideology*, p. 101.

16 Walter Laqueur, *Young Germany: A History of the German Youth Movement*, New York, 1962, p.41.

17 ibid., p. 6. For a concise portrait of the youth movement which draws

similar conclusions, see John De Graaf, "The Wandervogel," *CoEvolution Quarterly*, Fall 1977, pp. 14-21.

18   Reprinted in Ludwig Klages, *Sämtliche Werke*, Band 3, Bonn, 1974, pp. 614-630. No English translation is available.

19   Ulrich Linse, *Ökopax und Anarchie. Eine Geschichte der ökologischen Bewegungen in Deutschland*, München, 1986, p. 60.

20   Mosse, *The Crisis of German Ideology*, p. 211, and Laqueur, *Young Germany*, p. 34.

21   See Fritz Stern, *The Politics of Cultural Despair*, Berkeley, 1963.

22   Michael Zimmerman, *Heidegger's Confrontation with Modernity: Technology, Politics and Art*, Indianapolis, 1990, pp. 242-243.

23   See Michael Zimmerman, "Rethinking the Heidegger—Deep Ecology Relationship", *Environmental Ethics* vol. 15, no. 3 (Fall 1993), pp. 195-224.

24   Reproduced in Joachim Wolschke-Bulmahn, *Auf der Suche nach Arkadien*, München, 1990, p. 147.

25   Robert Pois, *National Socialism and the Religion of Nature*, London, 1985, p. 40.

26   ibid., pp. 42-43. The internal quote is taken from George Mosse, *Nazi Culture*, New York, 1965, p. 87.

27   Hitler, in Henry Picker, *Hitlers Tischgespräche im Führerhauptquartier 1941-1942*, Stuttgart, 1963, p. 151.

28   Adolf Hitler, *Mein Kampf*, München, 1935, p. 314.

29   Quoted in Gert Gröning and Joachim Wolschke-Bulmahn, "Politics, planning and the protection of nature: political abuse of early ecological ideas in Germany, 1933-1945", *Planning Perspectives* 2 (1987), p. 129.

30   Änne Bäumer, *NS-Biologie*, Stuttgart, 1990, p. 198.

31   Alfred Rosenberg, *Der Mythus des 20. Jahrhunderts*, München, 1938, p. 550. Rosenberg was, in the early years at least, the chief ideologist of the Nazi movement.

32   Picker, *Hitlers Tischgespräche*, pp. 139-140.

33 Quoted in Heinz Haushofer, *Ideengeschichte der Agrarwirtschaft und Agrarpolitik im deutschen Sprachgebiet,* Band II, München, 1958, p. 266.

34 See Dominick, *The Environmental Movement in Germany,* p. 107.

35 ibid., p. 113.

36 Bergmann, *Agrarromantik und Großstadtfeindschaft,* p. 334. Ernst Nolte makes a similar argument in *Three Faces of Fascism,* New York, 1966, pp. 407-408, though the point gets lost somewhat in the translation. See also Norbert Frei, *National Socialist Rule in Germany,* Oxford, 1993, p. 56: "The change in direction towards the 'soil' had not been an electoral tactic. It was one of the basic ideological elements of National Socialism . . ."

37 R. Walther Darré, *Um Blut und Boden: Reden und Aufsätze,* München, 1939, p. 28. The quote is from a 1930 speech entitled "Blood and Soil as the Foundations of Life of the Nordic Race."

38 Bramwell, *Ecology in the 20th Century,* p. 203. See also Frei, *National Socialist Rule in Germany,* p. 57, which stresses that Darré's total control over agricultural policy constituted a uniquely powerful position within the Nazi system.

39 Bergmann, *Agrarromantik und Großstadtfeindschaft,* p. 312.

40 ibid., p. 308.

41 See Haushofer, *Ideengeschichte der Agrarwirtschaft,* pp. 269-271, and Bramwell, *Ecology in the 20th Century,* pp. 200-206, for the formative influence of Steinerite ideas on Darré.

42 Haushofer, *Ideengeschichte der Agrarwirtschaft,* p. 271.

43 Anna Bramwell, "Darré. Was This Man 'Father of the Greens'?" *History Today,* September 1984, vol. 34, pp. 7-13. This repugnant article is one long series of distortions designed to paint Darré as an anti-Hitler hero -- an effort as preposterous as it is loathsome.

44 Roger Manvell and Heinrich Fraenkel, *Hess: A Biography,* London, 1971, p. 34.

45 Franz Neumann, *Behemoth. The Structure and Practice of National Socialism 1933-1944,* New York, 1944, p. 378.

46 Albert Speer, *Inside the Third Reich,* New York, 1970, p. 263.

47 ibid., p. 261.

48 Bramwell, *Ecology in the 20th Century,* p. 197.

49 Karl-Heinz Ludwig, *Technik und Ingenieure im Dritten Reich,* Düsseldorf, 1974, p. 337.

50 Quoted in Rolf Peter Sieferle, *Fortschrittsfeinde? Opposition gegen Technik und Industrie von der Romantik bis zur Gegenwart,* München, 1984, p. 220. Todt was just as convinced a Nazi as Darré or Hess; on the extent (and pettiness) of his allegiance to antisemitic policies, see Alan Beyerchen, *Scientists Under Hitler,* New Haven, 1977, pages 66-68 and 289.

51 Bramwell, *Blood and Soil,* p. 173.

52 Alwin Seifert, *Im Zeitalter des Lebendigen,* Dresden, 1941, p. 13. The book's title is grotesquely inapt considering the date of publication, it means "in the age of the living."

53 Alwin Seifert, *Ein Leben für die Landschaft,* Düsseldorf, 1962, p. 100.

54 Bramwell, *Ecology in the 20th Century,* p. 198. Bramwell cites Darré's papers as the source of the internal quote.

55 Seifert, *Ein Leben für die Landschaft,* p. 90.

56 William Shirer, *Berlin Diary,* New York, 1941, p. 19. Shirer also calls Hess Hitler's "protégé" (588) and "the only man in the world he fully trusts" (587), and substantiates Darré's and Todt's standing as well (590).

57 Quoted in Manvell and Fraenkel, *Hess,* p. 80. In a further remarkable confirmation of the 'green' faction's stature, Hitler once declared that Todt and Hess were "the only two human beings among all those around me to whom I have been truly and inwardly attached" (*Hess,* p. 132).

58 See Haushofer, *Ideengeschichte der Agrarwirtschaft,* p. 270, and Bramwell, *Ecology in the 20th Century,* p. 201.

59 ibid., pp. 197-200. Most of Todt's work also ran through Hess's office.

60 Raymond Dominick, "The Nazis and the Nature Conservationists", *The Historian* vol. XLIX no. 4 (August 1987), p. 534.

61   ibid., p. 536.

62   Hermand, *Grüne Utopien in Deutschland,* p. 114.

63   Dominick, "The Nazis and the Nature Conservationists", p. 529.

64   Gröning and Wolschke-Bulmahn, "Politics, planning and the protection of nature", p. 137.

65   ibid., p. 138.

66   Linse's *Ökopax und Anarchie,* among others, offers a detailed consideration of the history of eco-anarchism in Germany.

67   Pois, *National Socialism and the Religion of Nature,* p. 27.

68   Bramwell, *Ecology in the 20th Century,* p. 48.

"Ecology" and the Modernization
of Fascism in the German Ultra-right
Janet Biehl, 1993

1   On social ecology, see the many writings of Murray Bookchin, particularly *Remaking Society* (Boston: South End Press, 1989) and *Urbanization Without Cities* (Montreal: Black Rose Books, 1992).

2   Jutta Ditfurth, *Feuer in die Herzen: Plädoyer für eine Ökologische Linke Opposition* (Hamburg: Carlsen Verlag, 1992), part three, especially pp. 158, 172. Ditfurth was formerly a leading spokesperson for the leftists in the German Greens. Now that the Greens have lost their radicalism, she is currently involved in organizing the Ecological Left (Ökologische Linke) in Frankfurt.

3   George L. Mosse, "The Mystical Origins of National Socialism," *Journal of the History of Ideas*, vol. 22, no. 1 (Jan. 1961), p. 81. See also Jeffrey A. Goldstein, "On Racism and Anti-Semitism in Occultism and Nazism," *Yad Vashem Studies* 13, Livia Rothkirchen, ed. (Jerusalem: Yad Vashem, 1979), pp. 53-72.

4   George L. Mosse, *The Crisis of German Ideology: Intellectual Origins of the Third Reich* (New York: Grosset and Dunlap, Universal Library, 1964), p. 4.

5   On the *völkisch* movement, see Mosse, Crisis; Fritz Stern, *The Politics of Cultural Despair: A Study in the Rise of the Germanic Ideology* (Berkeley and Los Angeles: University of California Press, 1961); and Walter Z. Laqueur, *Young Germany: A History of the German Youth Movement* (New York: Basic Books, 1962).

6   Quoted in Ditfurth, *Feuer*, p. 170.

7   Wolfgang Haug, "'Pogromen beginnen im Kopf,'" *Schwarzer Faden: Vierteljahreschrift für Lust und Freiheit* [Grafenau]; translated as "'Pogroms Begin in the Mind,'" in *Green Perspectives*, no. 26 (May 1992).

8   Volkmar Wölk, "Neue Trends im ökofaschistischen Netzwerk: Am Beispiel der Anthroposophen, dem Weltbund zum Schutz des Lebens und der ÖDP," in *In bester Gesellschaft: Antifa-Recherche zwischen Konservatismus und Neo-faschismus*, Raimund Hethey and Peter Kratz, eds. (Göttingen: Verlag die Werkstatt, 1991). Wölk is a spokesperson for the VVN/Bund of Antifascists and has published widely on "neofascism."

9   Unless otherwise indicated, quotations in this section are from the National Revolutionaries" documents *Gegen Fremdherrschaft und Kapital and Grundsätze unseres Wollens—Die fünffache Revolution* (n.d.), as cited in Ditfurth, *Feuer*, pp. 228-30.

10   Walter Laqueur, *Germany Today: A Personal Report* (Boston: Little, Brown, 1985), p. 152. Also on Strasserite ideology, see Mosse, *Crisis*, pp. 286-90.

11   See Hans-Georg Betz, "On the German Question: Left, Right, and the Politics of National Identity," *Radical America*, vol. 20, no. 1 (1987), pp. 30-48.

12   See Betz, "On the German Question."

13   Henning Eichberg, "Produktivistische Mythen: Etwas über die Religion in der Industriekultur," in *Zurück zur Natur-Religion?* Holger Schleip, ed. (Freiburg: Hermann Bauer Verlag, 1986). Editor Schleip is, ironically, a member both of the Greens and of the *völkisch*-racist sect Deutsche Unitarier; the publisher, Hermann Bauer Verlag, is the largest New Age publisher in Germany. The content of Eichberg's article is summarized in

Wölk, "Neue Trends," p. 126.

14 Laqueur, *Germany Today*, p. 153. Laqueur cites Henning Eichberg,
    "Balkanisierung für jedermann," in the National Revolutionaries"
    periodical *Wir Selbst*, "a journal for national identity and international
    solidarity" (May-June 1983). The German right has been interested in the
    IRA since the 1920s; the title of this journal, *Wir Selbst* ("we ourselves"), is
    a translation of *Sinn Fein*.

15 See Betz, "On the German Question," pp. 45-46; and Wölk, "Neue
    Trends," p. 123.

16 Unless otherwise indicated, quotations in this section are from the FAP's
    Action Program (15 Aug. 1990); the FAP charter (15 Aug. 1989); "Basic
    Principles and Goals of the FAP—Electoral Program for Rhineland-
    Westphalia" (n.d.); and "Overview of Members of the Party Executive
    Committee for the Provincial Associations" (15 Aug. 1990), all as cited in
    Ditfurth, *Feuer*, p. 229ff. [Since early 1993, when this article was originally
    written, the FAP has been banned in the Federal Republic.]

17 See Christopher T. Husbands, "Militant Neo-Nazism in the Federal
    Republic of Germany in the 1960s," in *Neo-Fascism in Europe*, Luciano
    Cheles, Ronnie Ferguson, and Michalina Vaughan, eds. (Essex: Longman
    Group, UK Limited, 1991).

18 See Husbands, "Militant Neo-Nazism."

19 Husbands, "Militant Neo-Nazism," p. 96.

20 Quotations in this section are from the basic program of the Republicans,
    adopted at their first federal congress (26 Nov. 1983) in Munich; the
    1987 program of the Republicans; "Ja zu Europa—Nein zu dieser EG—
    Deutsche Interessen haben Vorrang," the Dinkelsbühl Declaration of
    the Republicans for the European elections of 1979; and the 1990 party
    program of the Republicans, all as cited in Ditfurth, *Feuer*, p. 228ff.

21 Unless otherwise indicated, quotations in this section are from the
    NPD's 1973 Düsseldorf program; the 1988 *Wurfsendung* of the NPD;

and the NPD newspaper *Deutsche Stimme* 4-5 (1992), all as cited in
Ditfurth, *Feuer*, p. 228ff. On the NPD generally, see David Childs, "The
Far Right in Germany Since 1945," in *Neo-Fascism in Europe*, Cheles,
Ferguson, and Vaughan, eds.

22 Betz, "On the German Question," p. 35.

23 Quotations in this section are from a DVU leaflet (c. 1990) and "Overview
of the Members of the Party Executive and the Provincial Associations"
(20 Nov. 1989), as cited in Ditfurth, *Feuer*, p. 228ff.

24 The following section on the root-race theory is based on Wölk, "Neue
Trends," pp. 120-21, and Ditfurth, *Feuer*, pp. 217-22. In English, a
mild "revised" account appears in Rudolf Steiner, *An Outline of Occult
Science* (Spring Valley, N.Y.: Anthroposophical Press, 1972), especially chap. 6.

25 Rudolf Steiner, lecture (3 March 1923), *Gesamtausgabe*, vol. 349, pp. 52-67,
cited in Ditfurth, *Feuer*, p. 221.

26 Steiner, *Outline*, p. 216.

27 Quoted in Ditfurth, *Feuer*, p. 216.

28 Quoted in Ditfurth, *Feuer*, p. 216.

29 Steiner, *Outline*, p. 361.

30 Ditfurth, *Feuer*, p. 200.

31 See Wölk, "Neue Trends," p. 123.

32 Ditfurth, *Feuer*, p. 222.

33 He is mentioned in passing in Laqueur, *Young Germany*, p. 194n.

34 Ditfurth, *Feuer*, p. 224.

35 Quoted in Betz, "On the German Question," p. 36.

36 Werner Georg Haverbeck, *Rudolf Steiner: Anwalt für
Deutschland* (Munich, 1989), pp. 143f, 242f, 324, cited in Ditfurth, *Feuer*,
pp. 224-26.

37 Werner Georg Haverbeck, "Das Ringen um Völker- und Geistesfreiheit,"
in *Europa* (Feb. 1990), p. 41f, cited in Wölk, "Neue Trends," pp. 131-32.

38 Wölk, "Neue Trends," p. 132.

39   Letter from the WSL's provincial executive for Schleswig-Holstein to the
     WSL presidium (28 July 1981), cited in Wölk, "Neue Trends," p. 133; also
     in *Vlothoer Tageblatt* (19 Nov. 1982), cited in Ditfurth, *Feuer*, p. 225.

40   Ursula Haverbeck-Wetzel, "Vom Wirtschaftskrieg zum Geisteskampf,"
     in *Europa* (Mar. 1990), p. 28, cited in Wölk, "Neue Trends," p. 132.

41   Helmut Roehrig, letter (2 Apr. 1982), cited in Wölk, "Neue Trends," p. 133.

42   Cited in Wölk, "Neue Trends," pp. 13-34. On Springmann in the Greens,
     see, e.g., Werner Hülsberg, *The German Greens: A Social and Political
     Profile*, trans. Gus Fagan (London and New York: Verso, 1988), pp. 94-95.

43   *Neue Anthropologie* 3-4 (1988), p. 91, cited in Wölk, "Neue Trends," p. 131.

44   Ditfurth, *Feuer*, p. 190.

45   See Conversation with Rudolf Bahro, "Die deutschen Linken und die
     nationale Frage oder unsere Ölinteressen am Golf," *Streitschrift 3* (Nov.
     1990), pp. 4-7, quoted in Ditfurth, *Feuer*, p. 210.

46   Conversation with Rudolf Bahro, *Streitschrift*, quoted in Roger Niedenführ,
     "New Age: Die spirituelle Rehabilitierung der Nationalsozialisten durch
     Rudolf Bahro, Rainer Langhans und J. Kirchoff," in *In bester Gesellschaft:
     Antifa-Recherche zwischen Konservatismus und Neo-faschismus*, Raimund
     Hethey and Peter Kratz, eds. (Göttingen: Verlag die Werkstatt, 1991), pp.
     141-54, at 149.

47   Niedenführ, "New Age," pp. 141-54, esp. 147-50.

48   Quoted in Hülsberg, *German Greens*, p. 93.

49   See the exchange between Bahro and André Gorz in *Telos*, no. 51 (Spring
     1982). See also Rudolf Bahro's *From Red to Green: Interviews with New
     Left Review*, trans. Gus Fagan and Richard Hurst (London: Verso, 1984),
     especially part three, wherein Bahro says, "In practice, if we want to
     build an ecological decentralized Germany, we have to first free German
     territory" (p. 237).

50   Bahro, From *Red to Green*, pp. 220-21.

51   Rudolf Bahro, "Hinein oder hinaus? Wozu steigen wir auf? Rede auf der

Bundesdelegiertenkonferenz der Grünen" (Hamburg), *Kommune* 1 (1985), pp. 40-43.

52 Conversation with Rudolf Bahro, "Die Deutschen," *Streitschrift*, quoted in Ditfurth, *Feuer*, p. 210.

53 Rudolf Bahro, *Connection* (July-Aug. 1989), quoted in Ditfurth, *Feuer*, pp. 207-08.

54 Lernwerkstatt, *Rundbrief* 13 (c. 1990); the Lernwerkstatt's 1991 program.

55 Rudolf Bahro, *Logik der Rettung: Wer kann die Apokalypse aufhalten? -- Ein Versuch über die Grundlagen ökologischer Politik* (Stuttgart and Vienna, 1987). I will refer to this book herein as *The Logic of Salvation*.

56 Conversation with Rudolf Bahro, "Die deutschen," *Streitschrift*, quoted in Ditfurth, *Feuer*, p. 210.

57 The author was present at this debate.

58 Rudolf Bahro, "Rette sich, wer kann," an interview with Rudolf Bahro, *Connection*, vol. 5, no. 8 (1989), pp. 18-19, cited in Niedenführ, "New Age," p. 148.

59 "Die Logik der Selbstausrottung," an interview with Rudolf Bahro, *Magazin 2000*, vol. 22, nos. 81-82 (1989), p. 64, cited in Niedenführ, "New Age," p. 148.

60 Niedenführ, "New Age," pp. 147-48.

61 Rudolf Bahro, "Lösung des Schattens und ökologische Kulturentwurf," *Connection*, vol. 6, no. 2 (1990), p. 65, cited in Niedenführ, "New Age," pp. 147-48.

62 Bahro, *Logik*, p. 153.

63 Bahro, *Logik*, p. 335; emphasis in the original.

64 Peter Kratz, "Bahros 'Grune Adolfs': Die 'Neue Rechte' an der Berliner Humboldt-Universität," reprinted in *A-Kurier* [Berlin] 41 (1993), pp. 6-15.

65 Bahro, *Logik*, p. 391.

66 Bahro, *Logik*, pp. 67-70. On the Conservative Revolution, see Stern, *Cultural Despair*, passim.

67 Conversation with Rudolf Bahro, "Die deutschen," *Streitschrift*, quoted in Ditfurth, *Feuer*, p. 210.

68 Kratz, "Bahros 'Grune Adolfs,'" p. 6.

69 Quoted in Dietmar Pieper, "Schickimicki unter Wolfen," *Der Spiegel* 26 (22 June 1992), pp. 62-63. See also Bahro, *Logik*, pp. 344, 481.

70 Rudolf Bahro, "Über kommunitäre Subsistenzwirtschaft und ihre Startbedingungen in die neuen Bundesländer," working paper, p. 10, cited in Kratz, "Bahros 'Grüne Adolfs,'" p. 9.

71 Bahro, *Logik*, p. 363.

72 "Salvation government" in Bahro, *Logik*; "god-state" in Pieper, "Schickimicki."

73 Bahro, *Logik*, p. 325.

74 Bahro, *Logik*, p. 491ff.

75 Bahro, *Logik*, p. 59.

76 Quoted in Ditfurth, *Feuer*, p. 206.

77 Conversation with Rudolf Bahro, "Die deutschen," *Streitschrift*, quoted in Kratz, "Bahros 'Grüne Adolfs,'" p. 8.

78 Bahro, *Logik*, p. 64.

79 Bahro, *Logik*, pp. 344-45.

80 Bahro, *Logik*, p. 346f. See also Robert Jungk, "Sein Kampf: Kritik an *Logik der Rettung*," in *tageszeitung* (10 Oct. 1987).

81 Bahro, *Logik*, p. 350.

82 Bahro, *Logik*, p. 461.

83 Bahro, *Logik*, p. 399.

84 Conversation with Rudolf Bahro, "Die deutschen," *Streitschrift*, p. 6, quoted in Kratz, "Bahros 'Grüne Adolfs,'" p. 8.

85 Conversation with Rudolf Bahro, "Die deutschen," *Streitschrift*, p. 6, quoted in Kratz, "Bahros 'Grüne Adolfs,'" p. 8.

86 Bahro, *Logik*, p. 347.

87 On the "sleeping emperor," see Norman Cohn, *The Pursuit of the*

Millennium: Revolutionary Millennarians and the Mystical Anarchists of the Middle Ages, rev. ed. (London and New York: Oxford University Press, 1970; original, 1961), chaps. 6-7.

88 Summarized by Niedenführ, "New Age," p. 149ff.

89 Rudolf Bahro, foreword to Jochen Kirchhoff, *Nietzsche, Hitler und die Deutschen: Die Perversion des Neuen Zeitalters* (Berlin, 1990), quoted in Niedenführ, "New Age," p. 150.

90 Bahro, foreword to Kirchhoff, *Nietzsche, Hitler*, quoted in Niedenführ, "New Age," p. 150.

91 Niedenführ, "New Age," p. 150.

92 Bahro, *Logik*, p. 346.

93 Rudolf Bahro, *Rückkehr: Die In-Welt Krise als Ursprung der Weltzerstörung* (Frankfurt: Horizonte Verlag/Berlin: Altis Verlag, 1991), pp. 24-25.

94 All Langhans's quotes are from Niedenführ, "New Age," p. 146.

95 Bahro, foreword to Kirchhoff, *Nietzsche, Hitler*, p. 26, cited in Niedenführ, "New Age," p. 152.

96 On Christophersen and Holocaust denial, see, for example, Roger Eatwell, "The Holocaust Denial: A Study in Propaganda Technique," in *Neo-Fascism in Europe*, Cheles, Ferguson, and Vaughan, eds.

97 This exchange was transcribed from a tape recording of the Bookchin-Bahro discussion, at which the author was present.

98 Quoted in Anti-EG Gruppe Köln, "Mit "LebensschützerInnen" und RassistInnen gegen EG und Kolonialismus? Anmerkungen zur ÖDP und anderen "BundnispartnerInnen" in der Kampagne '92," *ÖkoLinX: Zeitschrift der ökologischen Linken* 6 (July-Aug.-Sept. 1992), pp. 11 and 19, translated into English as "Should We Work in Coalition with 'Right-to-Lifers' and Racists?" *Green Perspectives*, no. 27 (Aug. 1992), pp. 2-6.

99 Daniel Gasman, *The Scientific Origins of National Socialism: Social Darwinism in Ernst Haeckel and the German Monist League* (New York:

American Elsevier; London: Macdonald & Co., 1971), pp. xxii-xxiii.

100 Adolf Hitler, *Mein Kampf*, trans. Ralph Mannheim (Boston: Houghton Mifflin, 1943), pp. 288, 400.

101 Gasman, *Scientific Origins*, p. xxiii.

102 For critiques of Gruhl, see: Anti-EG-Gruppe Köln, "Mit 'LebensschützerInnen'"; Antifa-Gruppe Freiburg und Volksfront gegen Reaktion, Faschismus und Krieg, eds., *Beitrag zur Kritik des Ökologismus*and *Beitrag zur Ideologie und Programmatik der ÖDP* (Cologne: GNN-Verlag, 1989); and Ditfurth, *Feuer*, pp. 151-69.

103 Herbert Gruhl, *Ein Planet wird geplündert* (reprint Frankfurt/Main, 1987; original, 1975).

104 Charlene Spretnak and Fritjof Capra, *Green Politics* (New York: E. P. Dutton, 1984), p. 15.

105 Ditfurth, *Feuer*, p. 152.

106 See, e.g., *tageszeitung* (7 Nov. 1991).

107 Quoted in Antifa-Gruppe Freiburg, *Beitrag*, p. 30.

108 Herbert Gruhl, *Das irdische Gleichgewicht* (Munich, 1985), p. 127; Antifa-Gruppe Freiburg, *Beitrag*, p . 27; and Anti-EG Gruppe Köln, "Mit 'LebensschützerInnen,'" p. 10.

109 Quoted in Antifa-Gruppe Freiburg, *Beitrag*, p. 35.

110 Antifa-Gruppe Freiburg, *Beitrag*, p. 68.

111 Quoted in Ditfurth, *Feuer*, p. 159.

112 Gruhl, *Ein Planet*, p. 322f.

113 Quoted in Antifa-Gruppe Freiburg, *Beitrag*, p. 114f.

114 Quoted in Anti-EG Gruppe Köln, "Mit 'LebensschützerInnen,'" p. 11.

115 Herbert Gruhl, "Die Menschheit ist am Ende," *Der Spiegel* 13 (1992), pp. 57-58.

116 Quoted in Anti-EG Gruppe Köln, "Mit 'LebensschützerInnen,'" p. 11.

117 Quoted in Anti-EG Gruppe Köln, "Mit 'LebensschützerInnen,'" p. 10.

118 Gruhl, *Ein Planet*, p. 110.

119 Herbert Gruhl, *Himmelfahrt ins Nichts* (Munich: Verlag Langen Müller, 1992), p. 242. See Thomas Ebermann's criticism, "Massakriert den Armen!" *Konkret* (June 1991), pp. 36-37, translated into English as "Massacre the Poor!" *Green Perspectives*, no. 27 (Aug. 1992), pp. 6-7.

120 Quoted in Antifa-Gruppe Freiburg, *Beitrag*, p. 113.

121 Quoted in Reimar Paul, "EK III in Grün-Braun," *Konkret* [Hamburg] (Dec. 1991), pp. 35-36.

122 Quoted in Paul, "EK III," pp. 35-36.

123 Tom Metzger, quoted in Elinor Langer, "The American Neo-Nazi Movement Today," *Nation* (16-23 July 1990), pp. 82-107, at 86.

124 Quoted in Langer, "American Neo-Nazi Movement," p. 86.

125 Bill Devall, *Simple in Means, Rich in Ends: Practicing Deep Ecology* (Layton, UT: Gibbs Smith, 1988), p. 189.

EPILOGUE—RIGHT-WING ECOLOGY IN GERMANY: ASSESSING THE HISTORICAL LEGACY
PETER STAUDENMAIER, 2011

1 Examples include Mark Neocleous, *Fascism* (University of Minnesota Press, 1997); Steve Chase, "Green Stormtroopers in the Streets of Berlin?" *Z Papers* October 1999; Kev Smith, "Ecofascism: Deep Ecology and Right-Wing Co-optation" *Synthesis/Regeneration* 32 (Fall 2003). For subsequent debates generated by the original edition of the book see the exchange on Rudolf Bahro in *Democracy and Nature* 11/12 (1998) and the exchange on ecofascism and neo-paganism in *The Pomegranate: Journal of Pagan Studies* 17/18 (2002).

2 Claudia Card, review of *Ecofascism* in *Ethics and the Environment* 1 (1996), 201-04; Ronald Creagh, review of *Ecofascism* in *Social Anarchism* 26 (1998).

3 The text originally appeared in the *Sydney Morning Herald*, November 13, 2003.

4   See e.g. David Orton's 2000 essay "Ecofascism: What is It? A Left
    Biocentric Analysis": http://home.ca.inter.net/~greenweb/Ecofascism.
    html. All internet sites cited here were accessed in December 2010.

5   A representative example is Gus di Zerega's 2010 essay "Environmentalism,
    NeoPaganism and EcoFascism: Here We Go Again": http://blog.beliefnet.
    com/apagansblog/2010/05/environmentalism-neopaganism-and-
    ecofascism-here-we-go-again.html

6   See David Watson, "Swamp Fever, Primitivism & the 'Ideological Vortex':
    Farewell to All That" *Fifth Estate* Fall 1997, as well as 'Nick Griffin',
    "National Anarchism: Trojan Horse for White Nationalism" *Green
    Anarchy* Spring 2005. Watson's essay is available online: http://www.
    insurgentdesire.org.uk/swampfever.htm

7   Michael Zimmerman, "The Threat of Ecofascism" *Social Theory and
    Practice* 21 (1995), 207-38; Zimmerman, "Ecofascism: A Threat to
    American Environmentalism?" in Roger Gottlieb, ed., *The Ecological
    Community* (Routledge, 1997), 229-54; Zimmerman, "Possible Political
    Problems of Earth-Based Religiosity" in Eric Katz, Andrew Light, and
    David Rothenberg, eds., *Beneath the Surface: Critical Essays on Deep
    Ecology* (MIT Press, 2000), 169-94; Zimmerman, "Ecofascism: An
    Enduring Temptation" in Zimmerman, ed., *Environmental Philosophy*
    (Prentice Hall, 2004), 390-408; Zimmerman, "Ecofascism" in Bron Taylor,
    ed., *Encyclopedia of Religion and Nature* (Continuum, 2005), 531-32.

8   One prominent example is the second chapter of Simon Schama,
    Landscape and Memory (New York: Vintage, 1996). A more detailed but
    less perspicacious account can be found in the chapter on "Nazi Ecology"
    in Luc Ferry, *The New Ecological Order* (University of Chicago Press,
    1995). Both works are committed to liberal assumptions and averse to
    radical political perspectives.

9   See e.g. Alston Chase, *In a Dark Wood: The Fight over Forests and the
    Rising Tyranny of Ecology* (Boston: Houghton Mifflin, 1995).

10 Cf. the entries in Taylor, ed., *Encyclopedia of Religion and Nature,* above all Roger Griffin, "Fascism," 639-44, as well as Nicholas Goodrick-Clarke, *Hitler's Priestess: Savitri Devi, the Hindu-Aryan Myth, and Neo-Nazism* (New York University Press, 1998), and Goodrick-Clarke, *Black Sun: Aryan Cults, Esoteric Nazism and the Politics of Identity* (New York University Press, 2002). The final chapter of *Hitler's Priestess,* on "Nazis, Greens, and the New Age," is especially apposite for enthusiasts of biocentrism, paganism, and esotericism.

11 Peter Zegers, "The Dark Side of Political Ecology" *Communalism* 3 (December 2002). On ecofascism in the UK see Derek Wall, "Darker Shades of Green"; http://another-green-world.blogspot.com/2006/05/darker-shades-of-green.html. On the US see Chip Berlet and Matthew Lyons, *Right-Wing Populism in America* (New York: Guilford, 2000), as well as the website of Political Research Associates, www.publiceye.org. Additional sources include Emanuel Sferios, "Population, Immigration, and the Environment: Eco-fascism and the environmental movement" *Z Magazine* June 1998; Heléne Lööw, "The Idea of Purity: The Swedish Racist Counterculture, Animal Rights, and Environmental Protection" in Jeffrey Kaplan and Heléne Lööw, eds., *The Cultic Milieu: Oppositional Subcultures in an Age of Globalization* (Rowman & Littlefield, 2002), 193-210; Jeff Shantz, "Scarcity and the Emergence of Fundamentalist Ecology" *Critique of Anthropology* 23 (2003), 144-54; Rajani Bhatia, "Green or Brown? White Nativist Environmental Movements" in Abby Ferber, ed., *Home-Grown Hate: Gender and Organized Racism* (Routledge, 2004), 194-213; "Browns and Greens" in Martin Lee, *The Beast Reawakens* (Routledge, 2000), 214-21; Roger Griffin, "Fascism's New Faces (and New Facelessness) in the 'post-fascist' Epoch" in Griffin, *A Fascist Century* (Palgrave Macmillan, 2008), 181-202.

12 For background on Tanton see Christopher Hayes, "Keeping America Empty: How one small-town conservationist launched today's anti-immigration movement" *In These Times* April 24, 2006, and Heidi Beirich,

"The Tanton Files: Nativist Leader's Racist Past Exposed" *Southern Poverty Law Center Intelligence Report* Winter 2008, as well as the website of the Institute for the Study of Academic Racism: http://www.ferris.edu/isar/. Further context is available in Peter Hay, "Green Political Thought: The Authoritarian and Conservative Traditions" in Hay, *Main Currents in Western Environmental Thought* (Indiana University Press, 2002), 173-93, and Eric Neumayer, "The environment: One more reason to keep immigrants out?" *Ecological Economics* 59 (2006), 204-07. On European far-right groups opposing immigration on environmental grounds see Stephan Faris, *Forecast: The Consequences of Climate Change* (New York: Holt, 2009), 62-94.

13   Cf. Gray Brechin, "Conserving The Race: Natural Aristocracies, Eugenics, and the U.S. Conservation Movement" *Antipode* 28 (1996), 229-45; Robert Gottlieb, *Forcing the Spring: The Transformation of the American Environmental Movement* (Island Press, 2005), 328-35; John Jackson and Nadine Weidman, *Race, Racism, and Science* (Rutgers University Press, 2006), 110-12; Alden Whitman, "Lindbergh and Conservation" *New York Times* June 23, 1969; Jonathan Spiro, *Defending the Master Race: Conservation, Eugenics, and the Legacy of Madison Grant* (University of Vermont Press, 2008).

14   Jonathan Olsen, *Nature and Nationalism: Right-Wing Ecology and the Politics of Identity in Contemporary Germany* (New York: St. Martin's, 1999) and Oliver Geden, *Rechte Ökologie: Umweltschutz zwischen Emanzipation und Faschismus* (Berlin: Elefanten, 1996).

15   Principal examples include Richard Stöss, *Vom Nationalismus zum Umweltschutz* (Opladen: Westdeutscher Verlag, 1980); Thomas Jahn and Peter Wehling, *Ökologie von rechts: Nationalismus und Umweltschutz bei der Neuen Rechten und den "Republikanern"* (Frankfurt: Campus, 1990); Volkmar Wölk, *Natur und Mythos: Ökologiekonzeptionen der 'Neuen' Rechten im Spannungsfeld zwischen Blut und Boden und New Age*

(Duisburg: Duisburger Institut für Sprach- und Sozialforschung, 1992);
Jürgen Wüst, *Konservatismus und Ökologiebewegung* (Frankfurt: Verlag
für interkulturelle Kommunikation, 1993); Justus H. Ulbricht, "Die
Heimat als Umwelt des Volkes: Ökologische Denkfiguren in Ideologie und
Programmatik 'neurechter' Organisationen" in Richard Faber, Hajo Funke,
and Gerhard Schoenberner, eds., *Rechtsextremismus: Ideologie und Gewalt*
(Berlin: Hentrich, 1995), 221-40; Ulrich Linse, "'Fundamentalistischer'
Heimatschutz: Die 'Naturphilosophie' Reinhard Falters" in Uwe Puschner
and Ulrich Großmann, eds., *Völkisch und national: Zur Aktualität
alter Denkmuster im 21. Jahrhundert* (Darmstadt: Wissenschaftliche
Buchgesellschaft, 2009), 156-78.

16   Cf. Dan Stone, "The Far Right and the Back-to-the-Land Movement" in
Julie Gottlieb and Thomas Linehan, eds., *The Culture of Fascism: Visions
of the Far Right in Britain* (London: Tauris, 2004), 182-98; Richard Moore-
Colyer, "Towards 'Mother Earth': Jorian Jenks, Organicism, the Right and
the British Union of Fascists" *Journal of Contemporary History* 39 (2004),
353-71; Graham Macklin, *Very Deeply Dyed in Black: Sir Oswald Mosley
and the Resurrection of British Fascism after 1945* (London: Tauris, 2007),
63-66; Matthew Jefferies and Mike Tyldesley, eds., *Rolf Gardiner: Folk,
Nature and Culture in Interwar Britain* (Farnham: Ashgate, 2011); see also
Richard Griffiths, *Fellow Travellers of the Right: British Enthusiasts for Nazi
Germany, 1933-39* (London: Constable, 1980), 142-46, 237-39, 317-28;
Dan Stone, "The Extremes of Englishness: The 'Exceptional' Ideology of
Anthony Mario Ludovici" *Journal of Political Ideologies* 4 (1999), 191-219;
Matthew Reed, "Fight the Future! How the Contemporary Campaigns of
the UK Organic Movement Have Arisen from their Composting of the
Past" *Sociologia Ruralis* 41 (2001), 131-45; Philip Conford, "Finance versus
Farming: Rural Reconstruction and Economic Reform, 1894–1955" *Rural
History* 13 (2002), 225-41; Dan Stone, "The English Mistery, the BUF, and
the Dilemmas of British Fascism" *Journal of Modern History* 75 (2003),

336-58; Philip Conford, "Organic Society: Agriculture and Radical Politics in the Career of Gerard Wallop, Ninth Earl of Portsmouth (1898-1984)" *Agricultural History Review* 53 (2005), 78-96.

17 On neo-paganism see Mattias Gardell, *Gods of the Blood: The Pagan Revival and White Separatism* (Duke University Press, 2003); Karla Poewe, "Scientific neo-paganism and the extreme right then and today" *Journal of Contemporary Religion* 14 (1999), 387-400; Betty Dobratz, "The Role of Religion in the Collective Identity of the White Racialist Movement" *Journal for the Scientific Study of Religion* 40 (2001), 287-301; Jeffrey Kaplan, *Radical Religion in America: Millenarian Movements from the Far Right to the Children of Noah* (Syracuse University Press, 1997); Horst Junginger, ed., *The Study of Religion under the Impact of Fascism* (Leiden: Brill, 2008); Andreas Speit, "Esoterik und Neuheidentum: Historische Allianzen und aktuelle Tendenzen" in Jens Mecklenburg, ed., *Handbuch deutscher Rechtsextremismus* (Berlin: Elefanten, 1996), 709-32; Eduard Gugenberger and Roman Schweidlenka, *Mutter Erde – Magie und Politik: Zwischen Faschismus und neuer Gesellschaft* (Vienna: Verlag für Gesellschaftskritik, 1987); Stefanie von Schnurbein, *Göttertrost in Wendezeiten: Neugermanisches Heidentum zwischen New Age und Rechtsradikalismus* (Munich: Claudius, 1993); Franziska Hundseder, *Wotans Jünger: Neuheidnische Gruppen zwischen Esoterik und Rechtsradikalismus* (Munich: Heyne, 1998); Hubert Cancik and Uwe Puschner, eds., *Antisemitismus, Paganismus, Völkische Religion* (Munich: Saur, 2004); Miro Jennerjahn, *Neue Rechte und Heidentum* (Frankfurt: Lang, 2006); Felix Wiedemann, *Rassenmutter und Rebellin: Hexenbilder in Romantik, völkischer Bewegung, Neuheidentum und Feminismus* (Würzburg: Königshausen & Neumann, 2007); Sandra Franz, *Die Religion des Grals: Entwürfe arteigener Religiosität im Spektrum von völkischer Bewegung, Lebensform, Okkultismus, Neuheidentum und Jugendbewegung* (Schwalbach: Wochenschau, 2009). The connections

between anthroposophy and ecofascism have been a primary subject of my own subsequent research, and I have detailed these connections elsewhere. See above all my article "Anthroposophy and Ecofascism" and its sequel, "The Art of Avoiding History" as well as two further articles co-authored with my colleague Peter Zegers, "Anthroposophy and its Defenders" and "The Janus Face of Anthroposophy," all available at www. social-ecology.org. For a more recent summary of the current state of research see Peter Staudenmaier, "Der deutsche Geist am Scheideweg: Anthroposophen in Auseinandersetzung mit völkischer Bewegung und Nationalsozialismus" in Uwe Puschner, ed., *Die Völkischreligiöse Bewegung im Nationalsozialismus* (Göttingen: Vandenhoeck & Ruprecht, forthcoming 2012). See also Jutta Ditfurth, *Entspannt in die Barbarei: Esoterik, (Öko-)Faschismus und Biozentrismus* (Hamburg: Konkret, 1996); Peter Bierl, *Wurzelrassen, Erzengel und Volksgeister: Die Anthroposophie Rudolf Steiners und die Waldorfpädagogik* (Hamburg: Konkret, 2005); Ingolf Christiansen, Rainer Fromm and Hartmut Zinser, *Brennpunkt Esoterik* (Hamburg 2006); Helmut Zander, *Anthroposophie in Deutschland: Theosophische Weltanschauung und gesellschaftliche Praxis 1884–1945* (Göttingen: Vandenhoeck & Ruprecht, 2007).

18 Pagan Liberation League, "Political Positions Outlined," January 7, 2000, copy in my possession. For context see Gardell, *Gods of the Blood*, 312-13, on explicit neo-pagan support for "ecofascism" and blood and soil politics. From the point of view of liberal and left neo-pagans, these pro-Nazi variants of paganism undoubtedly seem marginal, but they are not therefore neglible.

19 A particularly relevant example is the pamphlet by Kerry Bolton, *Rudolf Steiner & The Mystique of Blood & Soil: The Volkisch Views of the Founder of Anthroposophy* (Paraparaumu: Renaissance Press, 1999). Bolton lauds Steiner's contributions to the ecological strands of Nazism and notes that "racial evolution is the very basis of Anthroposophical teachings

on human spiritual development." (14) He also writes: "the Jewish preoccupation with 'measure, number and weight' naturally finds their emphasis on pursuits of a commercial nature, rather than those requiring spiritual impetus, such as the arts. Judaism is therefore seen by Steiner as *materialistic*, rooted in the physical, and its by-products are both capitalism and its mirror image, Marxism/Communism. His connection of Marxism and materialism with Judaism is another major belief he shared with the volkisch movement of the time." (12) Bolton's pamphlet on Steiner received a very favorable review by prominent neo-fascist Troy Southgate in his journal *Synthesis* in 2001.

20 See the instructive study by Graham Macklin, "Co-opting the counter culture: Troy Southgate and the National Revolutionary Faction" *Patterns of Prejudice* 39 (2005), 301-26. For North American viewpoints see *My Enemy's Enemy: Essays on globalization, fascism and the struggle against capitalism* (Montreal: Kersplebedeb, 2001) and *Confronting Fascism: Discussion Documents for a Militant Movement* (Montreal: Kersplebedeb, 2002). For illuminating context from an Italian perspective see Piero Ignazi, *Il polo escluso: Profilo storico del Movimento Sociale Italiano* (Bologna: Il Mulino, 1998), 190-91, and Dino Cofrancesco, "Faschismus: rechts oder links?" in Karl Dietrich Bracher and Leo Valiani, eds., *Faschismus und Nationalsozialismus* (Berlin: Duncker & Humblot, 1991), 41-106.

21 As in Germany, although the environmental strands in Italian Fascism were often overshadowed by countervailing tendencies toward industrialization and increasing mechanization in agriculture, the proto-ecological aspects of Fascist thought and policy should not be overlooked. For a range of perspectives compare Gustavo Corni, "Die Agrarpolitik des Faschismus: Ein Vergleich zwischen Deutschland und Italien" *Tel Aviver Jahrbuch für deutsche Geschichte* 17 (1988), 391-423; Alexander Nützenadel, *Landwirtschaft, Staat und Autarkie: Agrarpolitik im faschistischen Italien* (Tübingen: Niemeyer, 1997); Mauro Stampacchia,'*Ruralizzare L'Italia!'*

Agricoltura e bonifiche tra Mussolini e Serpieri (Milan: Angeli, 2000); James
Sievert, *The Origins of Nature Conservation in Italy* (New York: Lang, 2000),
193-214; Fabrizio Marasti, *Il fascismo rurale: Arrigo Serpieri e la bonifica
integrale* (Rome: Settimo Sigillo, 2001); Steen Bo Frandsen, "'The war that
we prefer': The Reclamation of the Pontine Marshes and Fascist Expansion"
in Gert Sørensen and Robert Mallett, eds., *International Fascism 1919-
1945* (Cass, 2002), 69-82; Peter Staudenmaier, "Fascism" in Shepard Krech
III, John McNeill, and Carolyn Merchant, eds., *Encyclopedia of World
Environmental History* (Routledge, 2004), 517-21; Mauro Stampacchia,
"Dalla bonifica alla guerra: la politica agraria del fascismo" in Angelo Moioli,
ed., *Con la vanga e col moschetto: Ruralità, ruralismo e vita quotidiana nella
RSI* (Venice: Marsilio, 2006), 103-11; Wilko Graf von Hardenberg, "A Brief
History of Access Rights and Environmental Conflicts in Fascist Italy" in
Marco Armiero and Marcus Hall, eds., *Nature and History in Modern Italy*
(Ohio University Press, 2010), 141-58. For an indication of the continuing
interest in the topic on the contemporary Italian far right see the preface by
Enzo Erra to Marasti, *Il fascismo rurale*, 5-11.

22 Giuseppe Tassinari, *Ten Years of Integral Land-Reclamation under the
Mussolini Act* (Faenza: Fratelli Lega, 1939), 14. This connection between
the "return to the soil" and the "health of the race" was reiterated in Fascist
publications; see e.g. "La mostra delle bonifiche" *Giornale d'Italia*, July 17,
1938, 8, and "La bonifica pontina e la politica razzista" *Giornale d'Italia*,
August 10, 1938, 2.

23 Cesare Longobardi, *Land-Reclamation in Italy: Rural Revival in the
Building of a Nation* (London: King, 1936), 3. The concurrent "battle of
grain," however, involved increased use of fertilizers and machinery.

24 Luciano Chimelli, "Prefazione all'edizione italiana" to Giovanni
Schomerus, *Il metodo di coltivazione biologico-dinamico* (Pergine: Torgler,
1934), xx. Cf. Luciano Chimelli, *Della lavorazione del terreno* (Pergine:
Torgler, 1941), and Chimelli, *Del governo dei concimi organici* (Trent:

Edizioni Mutilati e Invalidi, 1942). Chimelli was an anthroposophist and the primary representative of biodynamic agriculture in Fascist Italy.

25 Aldo Pavari, "Die Wiederbewaldung des Appenins" *Demeter*, February 1940, 13-17; for a similar celebration of Fascist environmental policy see Gerhard Reinboth, "Die italienischen Urbarmachungen" *Demeter*, July 1940, 66-67.

26 For background on the Thule Society cf. Hermann Gilbhard, *Die Thule-Gesellschaft: Vom okkulten Mummenschanz zum Hakenkreuz* (Munich: Kiessling, 1994) and Detlev Rose, *Die Thule-Gesellschaft: Legende, Mythos, Wirklichkeit* (Tübingen: Grabert, 1994).

27 My characterization of Hess as a Steinerite was based in part on the extent to which he structured his personal dietary and health choices around anthroposophical beliefs and biodynamic practices. My current view is that Hess's occult interests were too diffuse to be specifically identified as anthroposophical, and that he is better seen as a sympathizer of anthroposophy and the major sponsor of anthroposophical activities during the Nazi era, but not as an anthroposophist himself.

28 Gangolf Hübinger, "Die monistische Bewegung" in Hübinger, *Kultur und Kulturwissenschaften um 1900* vol. II (Stuttgart: Franz Steiner Verlag, 1997), 246-59. See also Frank Simon-Ritz, "Die freigeistige Bewegung im Kaiserreich" in Uwe Puschner, Walter Schmitz, and Justus Ulbricht, eds., *Handbuch zur 'Völkischen Bewegung' 1871-1918* (Munich: Saur, 1996), 208-23; Andreas Daum, *Wissenschaftspopularisierung im 19. Jahrhundert: Bürgerliche Kultur, naturwissenschaftliche Bildung und die deutsche Öffentlichkeit, 1848-1914* (Munich: Oldenbourg, 1998); Matthias Pilger-Strohl, "Eine deutsche Religion? Die freireligiöse Bewegung – Aspekte ihrer Beziehung zum völkischen Milieu" in Stefanie von Schnurbein and Justus Ulbricht, eds., *Völkische Religion und Krisen der Moderne: Entwürfe "arteigener" Glaubenssysteme seit der Jahrhundertwende* (Würzburg: Königshausen & Neumann, 2001), 342-66.

29   Major studies include Burkhardt Riechers, "Nature Protection during
National Socialism" *Historical Social Research* 21 (1996), 34-56; Karl Ditt,
"The Perception and Conservation of Nature in the Third Reich" *Planning
Perspectives* 15 (2001), 161-87; Joachim Radkau and Frank Uekötter,
eds., *Naturschutz und Nationalsozialismus* (Frankfurt: Campus, 2003);
Thomas Lekan, *Imagining the Nation in Nature: Landscape Preservation
and German Identity 1885-1945* (Harvard University Press, 2004); Franz-
Josef Brüggemeier, Mark Cioc, and Thomas Zeller, eds., *How Green were
the Nazis? Nature, Environment, and Nation in the Third Reich* (Ohio
University Press, 2005); Frank Uekoetter, *The Green and the Brown: A
History of Conservation in Nazi Germany* (Cambridge University Press,
2006); Willi Oberkrome, "Erhaltung und Gestaltung: Bemerkungen
zu Theorie und Praxis des Naturschutzes im nationalsozialistischen
Deutschland" in Hans-Werner Frohn and Friedemann Schmoll, eds.,
Natur und Staat: Staatlicher Naturschutz in Deutschland 1906-2006 (Bonn:
Bundesamt für Naturschutz, 2006), 315-41; Frank Uekötter, "Green
Nazis? Reassessing the Environmental History of Nazi Germany" *German
Studies Review* 30 (2007), 267-87. Balanced overviews of environmental
endeavors in Nazi Germany can be found in David Blackbourn, "Race and
Reclamation: National Socialism in Germany and Europe" in Blackbourn,
*The Conquest of Nature: Water, Landscape, and the Making of Modern
Germany* (New York: Norton, 2006), 251-309; Joachim Radkau, *Nature
and Power: A Global History of the Environment* (Cambridge University
Press, 2008), 260-65, and William Markham, *Environmental Organizations
in Modern Germany* (Oxford: Berghahn, 2008), 70-80.

30   See e.g. the editors' introduction to Brüggemeier, Cioc, and Zeller, eds.,
How Green were the Nazis, 15. For overviews of the recent historiography
see David Motadel, "The German Nature Conservation Movement in the
Twentieth Century" *Journal of Contemporary History* 43 (2008), 137-53;
Deborah Coen, "The Greening of German History" *Isis* 99 (2008), 142-

48; Marc Landry, "How Brown were the Conservationists? Naturism, Conservation, and National Socialism, 1900–1945" *Contemporary European History* 19 (2010), 83-93; and the forum on "The Nature of German Environmental History" in *German History* 27 (2009), 113-30.

31   For thorough historical background see Andreas Knaut, *Zurück zur Natur! Die Wurzeln der Ökologiebewegung* (Bonn: Arbeitsgemeinschaft Naturschutz, 1993) and Jost Hermand, *Old Dreams of a New Reich: Volkish Utopias and National Socialism* (Indiana University Press, 1993). For recent research on the various cultural precursors I briefly examined see Thomas Vordermayer, "Die Rezeption Ernst Moritz Arndts in Deutschland" *Vierteljahrshefte für Zeitgeschichte* 58 (2010), 483-508; Andrea Zinnecker, *Romantik, Rock und Kamisol: Volkskunde auf dem Weg ins Dritte Reich – Die Riehl-Rezeption* (Münster: Waxmann, 1996); Sabine Weißler, *Fokus Wandervogel: Der Wandervogel in seinen Beziehungen zu den Reformbewegungen vor dem Ersten Weltkrieg* (Marburg: Jonas, 2001); Ulrich Herrmann, ed., *"Mit uns zieht die neue Zeit": Der Wandervogel in der deutschen Jugendbewegung* (Weinheim: Juventa, 2006).

32   An empirically detailed example is John Alexander Williams, *Turning to Nature in Germany: Hiking, Nudism, and Conservation, 1900-1940* (Stanford University Press, 2007). Williams' approach is more complex than its reception would suggest; much of the book's argument is nuanced and perceptive. See also John Alexander Williams, "'The Chords of the German Soul are Tuned to Nature': The Movement to Preserve the Natural Heimat from the Kaiserreich to the Third Reich" *Central European History* 29 (1996), 339-84. Williams' book additionally contains important material on socialist variants of naturism in early twentieth century Germany, which along with anarchist and other radical approaches to environmental questions constitute a significant counterweight to the right-wing versions of 'turning to nature' examined here.

33   Dieter Buse, review of Williams, *Turning to Nature in Germany*, H-Net,

March 16, 2009.

34   Edward Ross Dickinson, "Not So Scary After All? Reform in Imperial and Weimar Germany" *Central European History* 43 (2010), 162.

35   Cf. William Rollins, *A Greener Vision of Home: Cultural Politics and Environmental Reform in the German Heimatschutz Movement, 1904-1918* (University of Michigan Press, 1997); Thomas Rohkrämer, *Eine andere Moderne? Zivilisationskritik, Natur und Technik in Deutschland 1880-1933* (Paderborn: Schöningh, 1999); Kevin Repp, *Reformers, Critics, and the Paths of German Modernity: Anti-politics and the Search for Alternatives, 1890-1914* (Harvard University Press, 2000); Matthew Jefferies, "Lebensreform: A Middle-Class Antidote to Wilhelminism?" in Geoff Eley and James Retallack, eds., *Wilhelminism and its Legacies: German Modernities, Imperialism, and the Meanings of Reform, 1890-1930* (Oxford: Berghahn, 2003), 91-106.

36   See Wolfgang Krabbe, "'Die Weltanschauung der Deutschen Lebensreformbewegung ist der Nationalsozialismus': Zur Gleichschaltung einer Alternativströmung im Dritten Reich" *Archiv für Kulturgeschichte* 71 (1989), 431-61; Uwe Puschner, "Lebensreform und völkische Weltanschauung" in Kai Buchholz, ed., *Die Lebensreform: Entwürfe zur Neugestaltung von Leben und Kunst um 1900* (Darmstadt: Häusser, 2001), 175-78; Ulrich Linse, "Völkisch-rassische Siedlungen der Lebensreform" in Puschner, Schmitz, and Ulbricht, eds., *Handbuch zur 'Völkischen Bewegung'*, 397-410; Gangolf Hübinger, "Der Verlag Eugen Diederichs in Jena: Wissenschaftskritik, Lebensreform und völkische Bewegung" *Geschichte und Gesellschaft* 22 (1996), 31-45; Oliver Piecha, "Anmerkungen zum Verhältnis zwischen Lebensreform und völkischem Fundamentalismus" in Sabine Kruse and Jürgen-Wolfgang Goette, eds., *Von Ascona bis Eden: Alternative Lebensformen* (Lübeck: Erich-Mühsam-Gesellschaft, 2006), 118-58; Willi Oberkrome, "Stamm und Landschaft: Heimatlicher Tribalismus und die Projektionen einer

'völkischen Neuordnung' Deutschlands 1920–1950" in Wolfgang

Hardtwig, ed., *Ordnungen in der Krise: Zur politischen Kulturgeschichte*

Deutschlands 1900-1933 (Munich: Oldenbourg, 2007), 69-94;

Wolfgang Krabbe, *Gesellschaftsveränderung durch Lebensreform:*

Strukturmerkmale einer sozialreformerischen Bewegung im Deutschland

der Industrialisierungsperiode (Göttingen: Vandenhoeck & Ruprecht,

1974); Janos Frecot, "Die Lebensreformbewegung" in Klaus Vondung,

ed., *Das wilhelminische Bildungsbürgertum: Zur Sozialgeschichte seiner*

Ideen (Göttingen: Vandenhoeck & Ruprecht, 1976), 138-52; Eva Barlösius,

Naturgemäße Lebensführung: Zur Geschichte der Lebensreform um die

Jahrhundertwende (Frankfurt: Campus, 1997); Janos Frecot, Johann

Friedrich Geist, and Diethart Kerbs, *Fidus, 1868 – 1948: Zur ästhetischen*

Praxis bürgerlicher Fluchtbewegungen (Hamburg: Rogner & Bernhard,

1997); Diethart Kerbs and Jürgen Reulecke, eds., *Handbuch der deutschen*

Reformbewegungen 1880-1933 (Wuppertal: Hammer, 1998); Bernd

Wedemeyer, "'Zum Licht': Die Freikörperkultur in der Wilhelminischen

Ära und der Weimarer Republik zwischen völkischer Bewegung,

Okkultismus und Neuheidentum" *Archiv für Kulturgeschichte* 81 (1999),

173-97; Uwe Puschner, *Die völkische Bewegung im wilhelminischen*

Kaiserreich: Sprache, Rasse, Religion (Darmstadt: Wissenschaftliche

Buchgesellschaft, 2001); Bernd Wedemeyer-Kolwe, *"Der neue Mensch":*

Körperkultur im Kaiserreich und in der Weimarer Republik (Würzburg:

Königshausen & Neumann, 2004); Florentine Fritzen, *Gesünder Leben: Die*

Lebensreformbewegung im 20. Jahrhundert (Stuttgart: Franz Steiner Verlag,

2006); Stefan Breuer, *Die Völkischen in Deutschland: Kaiserreich und*

Weimarer Republik (Darmstadt: Wissenschaftliche Buchgesellschaft, 2008).

37 For a variety of viewpoints see Richard Wolin, *The Politics of Being: The*

Political Thought of Martin Heidegger (Columbia University Press, 1990),

Tom Rockmore, *On Heidegger's Nazism and Philosophy* (University of

California Press, 1992), Hugo Ott, *Martin Heidegger: A Political Life*

(Harper Collins, 1993), Hans Sluga, *Heidegger's Crisis: Philosophy and Politics in Nazi Germany* (Harvard University Press, 1993), *Bernd Martin*, ed., *Martin Heidegger und das 'Dritte Reich'* (Darmstadt: Wissenschaftliche Buchgesellschaft, 1989), Dieter Thomä, ed., *Heidegger-Handbuch: Leben, Werk, Wirkung* (Stuttgart: Metzler, 2003), Bernhard Taureck, ed., *Politische Unschuld? In Sachen Martin Heidegger* (Munich: Fink, 2008). Curiously, the best that Heidegger's defenders seem to be able to say about the political value of his philosophy is that it is hypothetically commensurable with "a commitment to orthodox liberal democracy." (Julian Young, *Heidegger, philosophy, Nazism*, Cambridge University Press, 1997, 5) Perhaps this should be cause for reflection among Heidegger's admirers on the left. Some critics of Heidegger fall into the obverse error by viewing his rejection of liberalism as Heidegger's cardinal sin, philosophically and politically, and concluding that the indelible taint of Heideggerianism ruins the work of thinkers as diverse as Marcuse, Arendt, Sartre, Jonas, Löwith, and Levinas. What might help move the debate forward is a philosophically informed and politically radical critique of Heidegger's ideas as a specific instance of German right-wing thought, a critique that is satisfied neither with conformist liberalism nor with vacuous theoretical eclecticism.

38   Cf. Theodor Adorno, *The Jargon of Authenticity* (Northwestern University Press, 1973), Pierre Bourdieu, *The Political Ontology of Martin Heidegger* (Stanford University Press, 1991), Charles Bambach, *Heidegger's Roots: Nietzsche, National Socialism, and the Greeks* (Cornell University Press, 2003), Daniel Morat, *Von der Tat zur Gelassenheit: Konservatives Denken bei Martin Heidegger, Ernst Jünger und Friedrich Georg Jünger 1920-1960* (Göttingen: Wallstein, 2007).

39   Consider, for example, the contrasts between Robert Richards' work and Richard Weikart's work. Weikart, an intelligent design proponent, has produced historical scholarship which for all its flaws rightly points to the racist strands in Haeckel's thought, while Richards' otherwise impeccable

scholarship badly misjudges this point, despite the fact that Richards' work
is of much less dubious provenance than Weikart's; Richards' argument
amounts to an apologia for and indeed denial of Haeckel's antisemitism
and racism. Cf. Richard Weikart, *From Darwin to Hitler: Evolutionary
Ethics, Eugenics, and Racism in Germany* (New York: Palgrave, 2004),
Robert Richards, *The Tragic Sense of Life: Ernst Haeckel and the Struggle
over Evolutionary Thought* (University of Chicago Press, 2008), and Robert
Richards, "Ernst Haeckel's Alleged Anti-Semitism and Contributions to
Nazi Biology" *Biological Theory* 2 (2007), 97-103. For an earlier version
of the apologetic approach to Haeckel see Alfred Kelly, *The Descent
of Darwin: The Popularization of Darwinism in Germany, 1860-1914*
(University of North Carolina Press, 1981). More informative treatments
of Haeckel's racial views can be found in Jürgen Sandmann, *Der Bruch
mit der humanitären Tradition: die Biologisierung der Ethik bei Ernst
Haeckel und anderen Darwinisten seiner Zeit* (Stuttgart: Fischer, 1990),
Uwe Hoßfeld, *Geschichte der biologischen Anthropologie in Deutschland*
(Stuttgart: Steiner, 2005), 144-59, and John Haller, "The Species Problem:
Nineteenth-Century Concepts of Racial Inferiority in the Origin of Man
Controversy" *American Anthropologist* 72 (1970), 1319-29.

40 The second edition of Gasman's *The Scientific Origins of National
Socialism: Social Darwinism in Ernst Haeckel and the German Monist
League* (New Brunswick: Transaction, 2004) reprints the original text
unrevised but includes a substantial new introduction responding to
criticisms. Gasman's other book, *Haeckel's Monism and the Birth of
Fascist Ideology* (New York: Lang, 1998), contains a wealth of important
information though its arguments are often highly overstated and
oversimplified. As Roger Griffin notes, Haeckel's Monism "was just one of
many totalizing cosmologies of decadence and rebirth which helped shape
the cultural climate of the *fin-de-siècle* in which fascism's palingenetic
fantasies first crystallized as a rudimentary political vision." (Griffin,

"Fascism" in Taylor, ed., *Encyclopedia of Religion and Nature*, 643) For further context cf. Jackson and Weidman, *Race, Racism, and Science*, 85-88 and 120-25; Günter Altner, "Der Sozialdarwinismus" in Altner, ed., *Der Darwinismus: Die Geschichte einer Theorie* (Darmstadt: Wissenschaftliche Buchgesellschaft, 1981), 95-99; Paul Weindling, *Health, Race, and German Politics between National Unification and Nazism, 1870-1945* (Cambridge University Press, 1989); Paul Crook, "Social Darwinism: The Concept" *History of European Ideas* 22 (1996), 261-74; Mike Hawkins, *Social Darwinism in European and American thought, 1860-1945* (Cambridge University Press, 1997); Richard Evans, "In Search of German Social Darwinism: The History and Historiography of a Concept" in Manfred Berg and Geoffrey Cocks, eds., *Medicine and Modernity: Public Health and Medical Care in Nineteenth- and Twentieth-Century Germany* (Cambridge University Press, 1997), 55-79; Paul Weindling, "Dissecting German Social Darwinism: Historicizing the Biology of the Organic State" *Science in Context* 11 (1998), 619-37; Kurt Bayertz, "Darwinismus als Politik: Zur Genese des Sozialdarwinismus in Deutschland 1860-1900" in Erna Aescht, ed., *Welträtsel und Lebenswunder: Ernst Haeckel - Werk, Wirkung und Folgen* (Linz: Oberösterreichisches Landesmuseum, 1998), 229-88; Uwe Hoßfeld, "Haeckelrezeption im Spannungsfeld von Monismus, Sozialdarwinismus und Nationalsozialismus" *History and Philosophy of the Life Sciences* 21 (1999), 195-213; Peter Bowler, *Evolution: The History of an Idea* (University of California Press, 2003); André Pichot, *The Pure Society: From Darwin to Hitler* (Verso, 2009); Peter Bowler, "The Eclipse of Pseudo-Darwinism? Reflections on Some Recent Developments in Darwin Studies" *History of Science* 47 (2009), 431-43.

41 Some of the most insightful historians of the German right have raised significant reservations about a "culturalist approach" to understanding the heterogeneous assortment of right-wing groups and worldviews in the decades before 1933. I see the topic as a prime opportunity for integrating

intellectual and institutional history. For a trenchant critique of several common frameworks see Geoff Eley, "Origins, Post-Conservatism, and the History of the Right" *Central European History* 43 (2010), 327-39. A superb overview can be found in Stefan Breuer, *Ordnungen der Ungleichheit - die deutsche Rechte im Widerstreit ihrer Ideen 1871-1945* (Darmstadt: Wissenschaftliche Buchgesellschaft, 2001). In addition to the studies cited above and in the original edition of *Ecofascism*, English-speaking readers interested in the broad cultural background may consult the following works: Detlev Peukert, "Nazi Germany and the pathologies and dislocations of modernity" in Peukert, *Inside Nazi Germany* (Yale University Press, 1987), 243-49; Hermann Glaser, *The Cultural Roots of National Socialism* (University of Texas Press, 1978); Roderick Stackelberg, *Idealism Debased: From völkisch Ideology to National Socialism* (Kent State University Press, 1981); Gary Stark, *Entrepreneurs of Ideology: Neoconservative Publishers in Germany, 1890-1933* (University of North Carolina Press, 1981); Jeffrey Herf, *Reactionary Modernism: Technology, Culture, and Politics in Weimar and the Third Reich* (Cambridge University Press, 1984); Martin Green, *Mountain of Truth: The Counterculture Begins, Ascona, 1900-1920* (University Press of New England, 1986); Nicholas Goodrick-Clarke, *The Occult Roots of Nazism: The Ariosophists of Austria and Germany, 1890-1935* (New York University Press, 1992); Anne Harrington, *Reenchanted Science: Holism in German Culture from Wilhelm II to Hitler* (Princeton University Press, 1996); Colin Riordan, ed., *Green Thought in German Culture: Historical and Contemporary Perspectives* (University of Wales Press, 1997); Michael Hau, *The Cult of Health and Beauty in Germany: A Social History, 1890-1930* (University of Chicago Press, 2003); George Williamson, *The Longing for Myth in Germany: Religion and Aesthetic Culture from Romanticism to Nietzsche* (University of Chicago Press, 2004); Christof Mauch, ed., *Nature in German History* (Oxford: Berghahn, 2004); Thomas Lekan and Thomas Zeller, eds.,

Germany's Nature: New Approaches to Environmental History (Rutgers University Press, 2005).

42 See e.g. Thomas Rohkrämer, "Bewahrung, Neugestaltung, Restauration? Konservative Raum- und Heimatvorstellungen in Deutschland 1900–1933" in Hardtwig, ed., *Ordnungen in der Krise*, 66.

43 Hermand, *Grüne Utopien in Deutschland*, 112-18. The term 'ecofascism', on the other hand, can be found in Murray Bookchin's work from the 1970s and was already current in the literature when the original edition of this book appeared, and had in fact been used a decade earlier by left environmentalists critical of the authoritarian and Malthusian strands in contemporary ecological politics; see the section titled "Ecofascism" in David Pepper, *The Roots of Modern Environmentalism* (Routledge, 1986), 204-13.

44 Robert Proctor, *The Nazi War on Cancer* (Princeton University Press, 1999), 5.

45 On the status of animals in Nazi ideology and practice see the sophisticated study by Boria Sax, *Animals in the Third Reich* (Continuum, 2000). A judicious appraisal of Hitler's vegetarianism is available in Fritzen, *Gesünder Leben*, 227-29 and 219; see also 64-106 on the history of *Lebensreform* efforts between 1933 and 1945, particularly vegetarianism and natural healing methods. Nazi officials followed a similar course with vegetarian organizations as they did with other *Lebensreform* groups, co-opting some while suppressing others. Several vegetarian societies received official sanction in 1933 and 1934 and were incorporated into the Nazi *Lebensreform* apparatus; other vegetarian groups were either folded into the officially sanctioned ones or shut down. Nazi *Lebensreform* organs continued to promote vegetarianism into the late 1930s. On Nazi support for natural healing cf. Robert Proctor, *Racial Hygiene: Medicine under the Nazis* (Harvard University Press, 1988), 223-50; Walter Wuttke-Groneberg, "Nationalsozialistische Medizin: Volks- und Naturheilkunde auf 'neuen Wegen'" in Heinz Abholz, ed., *Alternative Medizin* (Berlin 1983), 27-50; Detlef Bothe, *Neue Deutsche Heilkunde 1933–1945*

(Husum 1991); Doris Kratz, *Die Heilkunde in der Zeit der Weimarer Republik - Die 'angepaßte' Medizin in der Zeit der NS-Diktatur* (Berlin 2004); Daniela Angetter, "Alternativmedizin kontra Schulmedizin im Nationalsozialismus" in Judith Hahn, ed., *Medizin im Nationalsozialismus und das System der Konzentrationslager* (Frankfurt 2005); Uwe Heyll, *Wasser, Fasten, Luft und Licht: Die Geschichte der Naturheilkunde in Deutschland* (Frankfurt 2006), 229-69.

46 Thomas Zeller, "Molding the Landscape of Nazi Environmentalism: Alwin Seifert and the Third Reich" in Brüggemeier, Cioc, and Zeller, eds., *How Green were the Nazis*, 148. See also Zeller, "'Ganz Deutschland sein Garten': Alwin Seifert und die Landschaft des Nationalsozialismus" in Radkau and Uekötter, eds., *Naturschutz und Nationalsozialismus*, 273-307; Charlotte Reitsam, *Das Konzept der 'bodenständigen Gartenkunst' Alwin Seiferts* (Frankfurt: Lang, 2001); Gert Gröning and Joachim Wolschke-Bulmahn, *Grüne Biographien: Biographisches Handbuch zur Landschaftsarchitektur des 20. Jahrhunderts in Deutschland* (Berlin: Patzer, 1997), 361-63; Franz Seidler, *Fritz Todt: Baumeister des Dritten Reiches* (Berlin: Herbig, 1986), 116-20, 279-85; Joachim Wolschke-Bulmahn, "Biodynamischer Gartenbau, Landschaftsarchitektur und Nationalsozialismus" *Das Gartenamt*, September 1993, 590-95, and October 1993, 638-42; Willi Oberkrome, *Deutsche Heimat: Nationale Konzeption und regionale Praxis von Naturschutz, Landschaftsgestaltung und Kulturpolitik in Westfalen-Lippe und Thüringen (1900-1960)* (Paderborn: Schöningh, 2004).

47 Compare Joachim Wolschke-Bulmahn, "Political Landscapes and Technology: Nazi Germany and the Landscape Design of the *Reichsautobahnen*" *CELA Annual Conference Papers* 1995; William Rollins, "Whose Landscape? Technology, Fascism, and Environmentalism on the National Socialist Autobahn" *Annals of the Association of American Geographers* 85 (1995), 494-520; Dietmar Klenke, "Autobahnbau und Naturschutz in Deutschland: Eine Liaison von Nationalpolitik,

Landschaftspflege und Motorisierungsvision bis zur ökologischen Wende der siebziger Jahre" in Matthias Frese and Michael Prinz, eds., *Politische Zäsuren und gesellschaftlicher Wandel im 20. Jahrhundert* (Paderborn: Schöningh, 1996), 465-98; Jochen Zimmer, "Politische Landschaften: Reichsautobahnbau und Autobahnmalerei" in Christof Stracke, ed., *Soziologie als Krisenwissenschaft* (Münster: Lit, 1998), 206-19; Erhard Schütz, *Mythos Reichsautobahn: Bau und Inszenierung der Straßen des Führers 1933-1941* (Berlin: Links, 2000); Thomas Zeller, *Driving Germany: The Landscape of the German Autobahn, 1930-1970* (Oxford: Berghahn, 2007); Charlotte Reitsam, *Reichsautobahn-Landschaften im Spannungsfeld von Natur und Technik* (Saarbrücken: Müller, 2009).

48 In a July 11, 1949 letter to the appeals court, Seifert claimed that he had been "unwillingly" made a member of the NSDAP, and his lawyer wrote on June 28, 1950 that Hess had enlisted Seifert in the party "without his knowledge." Both letters are in Seifert's file at the Staatsarchiv München, Spruchkammerakte Ka. 1511. Documents from the Nazi era disprove these claims. On his December 18, 1940 application to the *Reichsschrifttumskammer*, for example, Seifert stated plainly that he was an NSDAP member; see Bundesarchiv Berlin (hereafter BA), RK/B185: 2300. Hess's letters to Seifert address him as "Lieber Parteigenosse Seifert," e.g. Rudolf Hess to Alwin Seifert, November 14, 1938, BA R58/6223/1: 318; see also Seifert to Hess, May 10, 1937, Institut für Zeitgeschichte, Munich, ED 32/422/1952: 101. For context on Seifert's party membership see Reitsam, *Das Konzept der 'bodenständigen Gartenkunst' Alwin Seiferts*, 21, 25-26.

49 See the April 4, 1944 letter from the *Organisation Todt* to Seifert designating him an *Einsatzleiter* ("erster Generalsrang"), Staatsarchiv München, Spruchkammerakte Ka. 1511. At his de-Nazification trial Seifert claimed that the promotion, granted to facilitate his work in German-occupied Italy, was reversed by higher authorities.

50 In addition to the texts cited in my chapter on the 'green wing,' examples

include Alwin Seifert, "Natur als harmonisches Ganzes" *Leib und Leben*, May 1937, 115-17; Seifert, "Von der Muttererde" *Der Schulungsbrief: Das zentrale Monatsblatt der NSDAP*, November 1938, 373-77; Seifert, "Die Zukunft der ostdeutschen Landschaft" *Die Strasse*, December 1939, 633-36; Seifert, "Die lebensgesetzliche Landbauweise" *Die Strasse*, August 1940, 350; Seifert, "Die Wiedergeburt landschaftsgebundenen Bauens" *Die Strasse*, September 1941, 286-89; Seifert, "Über naturnahen Gartenbau" *Leib und Leben*, August 1942, 67-69. For a detailed sense of Seifert's dual commitment to National Socialism and to organic agriculture see his May 1941 manifesto "Die bäuerlich-unabhängige Landbauweise," Bundesarchiv Koblenz (hereafter BAK), N1094/II/1.

51 Gröning and Wolschke-Bulmahn, *Grüne Biographien*, 358. His publications include Max Karl Schwarz, "Biologisch-dynamische Wirtschaftsweise unter Berücksichtigung ihres Wertes für den Gartengedanken" *Gartenkunst*, October 1930, 167-70; Schwarz, "Zum Siedlungsproblem" *Demeter*, October 1931, 180-85; Schwarz, *Ein Weg zum praktischen Siedeln* (Düsseldorf: Pflugschar-Verlag, 1933); Schwarz, "Betriebsorganismen an der Reichsautobahn" *Die Strasse*, December 1939, 659-62; Schwarz, "Zum Grünaufbau im ostdeutschen Raum" *Die Strasse*, April 1940, 150-54; Schwarz, "Zeitgemäße Gedanken über Garten- und Landschaftsgestaltung" *Gartenbau im Reich*, June 1942, 94-95; Schwarz, "Ein Vorschlag zur biologischen Regelung der städtischen Abfallwirtschaft" *Leib und Leben*, December 1942, 108-09.

52 Schwarz reportedly converted Robert Ley's estate to biodynamic format; see Seifert to Darré, June 12, 1941, BAK N1094/II/1. A further member of Seifert's coterie of landscape advocates, Hinrich Meyer-Jungclaussen, was also a supporter of biodynamics; cf. BA R58/6197/1: 194 and BA R58/6144/2: 109.

53 Cf. Gert Gröning and Joachim Wolschke-Bulmahn, *Der Drang nach Osten: Zur Entwicklung der Landespflege im Nationalsozialismus und während des*

Zweiten Weltkrieges in den "eingegliederten Ostgebieten" (Munich: Minerva, 1987); Marie-Luise Heuser, "Was grün begann endete blutigrot: Von der Naturromantik zu den Reagrarisierungs- und Entvölkerungsplänen der SA und SS" in Dieter Hassenpflug, ed., *Industrialismus und Ökoromantik: Geschichte und Perspektiven der Ökologisierung* (Wiesbaden: Deutscher Universitäts-Verlag, 1991), 43-64; Stefan Körner, *Der Aufbruch der modernen Umweltplanung in der nationalsozialistischen Landespflege* (Berlin: Technische Universität, 1995); Michael Hartenstein, *Neue Dorflandschaften: Nationalsozialistische Siedlungsplanung in den "eingegliederten Ostgebieten" 1939 bis 1944* (Berlin: Köster, 1998); Uwe Mai, *Rasse und Raum: Agrarpolitik, Sozial- und Raumplanung im NS-Staat* (Paderborn: Schöningh, 2002); Joachim Wolschke-Bulmahn and Gert Gröning, "Zum Verhältnis von Landschaftsplanung und Nationalsozialismus: Dargestellt an Entwicklungen während des Zweiten Weltkriegs in den 'eingegliederten Ostgebieten'" in *Naturschutz hat Geschichte* (Essen: Klartext, 2003), 163-92; Isabel Heinemann, *"Rasse, Siedlung, deutsches Blut": Das Rasse- und Siedlungshauptamt der SS und die rassenpolitische Neuordnung Europas* (Göttingen: Wallstein, 2003).

54 See Michael Imort, "'Eternal Forest – Eternal *Volk*': The Rhetoric and Reality of National Socialist Forest Policy" in Brüggemeier, Cioc, and Zeller, eds., *How Green were the Nazis*, 43-72; Johannes Zechner, "'Die grünen Wurzeln unseres Volkes': Zur ideologischen Karriere des 'deutschen Waldes'" in Puschner and Großmann, eds., *Völkisch und national*, 179-94; Heinrich Rubner, *Deutsche Forstgeschichte 1933 - 1945: Forstwirtschaft, Jagd und Umwelt im NS-Staat* (St. Katharinen: Scripta Mercaturae, 1997); Robert Lee and Sabine Wilke, "Forest as *Volk*: *Ewiger Wald* and the Religion of Nature in the Third Reich" *Journal of Social and Ecological Boundaries* 1 (2005), 21-46; Johannes Zechner, *"Ewiger Wald und ewiges Volk": Die Ideologisierung des deutschen Waldes im Nationalsozialismus* (Munich: Technische Universität, 2006); Oliver Rathkolb, Maria Wirth, and Michael Wladika, *Die*

"Reichsforste" in Österreich 1938-1945: Arisierung, Restitution, Zwangsarbeit und Entnazifizierung (Vienna: Böhlau, 2010). For sources from the Nazi era see Franz Heske, *German Forestry* (Yale University Press, 1938) and Adalbert Ebner, *German Forests: Treasures of a Nation* (New York: German Library of Information, 1940).

55 For thoughtful general reflections on the politics of organic agriculture see Pernille Kaltoft, "Values about Nature in Organic Farming Practice and Knowledge" *Sociologia Ruralis* 39 (1999), 39-53; Jack Kloppenburg, Sharon Lezberg, Kathryn De Master, George Stevenson, John Hendrickson, "Tasting Food, Tasting Sustainability: Defining the Attributes of an Alternative Food System with Competent, Ordinary People" *Human Organization* 59 (2000), 177-86; Timothy Vos, "Visions of the middle landscape: Organic farming and the politics of nature" *Agriculture and Human Values* 17 (2000), 245-56; Julie Guthman, *Agrarian Dreams: The Paradox of Organic Farming in California* (University of California Press, 2004); Steven Stoll, "The Smallholder's Dilemma" *Technology and Culture* 47 (2006), 808-13; Warren Belasco, *Appetite for Change: How the Counterculture took on the Food Industry* (Cornell University Press, 2007); Julie Guthman, "Commentary on Teaching Food: Why I am Fed Up with Michael Pollan et al" *Agriculture and Human Values* 24 (2007), 261-64; Raj Patel, *Stuffed and Starved: The Hidden Battle for the World Food System* (New York: Melville House, 2008), 244-48 and 305-10; Jordan Kleiman, "Local Food and the Problem of Public Authority" *Technology and Culture* 50 (2009), 399-417; Matthew Reed, *Rebels for the Soil: The Rise of the Global Organic Food and Farming Movement* (London: Earthscan, 2010); as well as two unpublished texts: the 2008 essay "The Politics of Organic Farming" by Laura Sayre of Yale University's Program in Agrarian Studies, and the 2009 study "Going Loco: The Cultural and Political Meaning of the U.S. Local Foods Movement" by my colleague Chaia Heller of the Instiitute for Social Ecology. For a recent argument linking sustainable agricultural initiatives to broader struggles

for social and ecological justice see Carmelo Ruiz-Marrero, "Organic and Beyond" *Counterpunch*, January 14, 2011.

56 The initial reception of Bramwell's book was partly positive; see e.g. the review of *Blood and Soil* by John Farquharson in *German History 3* (1986), 95-97. More critical appraisals of her work include Gustavo Corni and Herbert Gies, *'Blut und Boden': Rassenideologie und Agrarpolitik im Staat Hitlers* (Idstein: Schulz-Kirchner, 1994); Piers Stephens, "Blood, Not Soil: Anna Bramwell and the Myth of 'Hitler's Green Party'" *Organization & Environment* 14 (2001), 173-87; Gesine Gerhard, "Richard Walther Darré – Naturschützer oder 'Rassenzüchter'?" in Radkau and Uekötter, eds., *Naturschutz und Nationalsozialismus*, 257-71; Gesine Gerhard, "Breeding Pigs and People for the Third Reich: Richard Walther Darré's Agrarian Ideology" in Brüggemeier, Cioc, and Zeller, eds., *How Green were the Nazis*, 129-46. For a keen critique of Bramwell's book from a politically radical perspective see the pamphlet by J. Sakai, *The Green Nazi: An investigation into fascist ecology* (Montreal: Kersplebedeb, 2002). The broader literature on Nazi agricultural policy is extensive; see J.E. Farquharson, *The Plough and the Swastika: The NSDAP and Agriculture in Germany, 1928-45* (London: Sage, 1976); Friedrich Grundmann, *Agrarpolitik im 'Dritten Reich'* (Hamburg: Hoffmann und Campe, 1979); Jan Smit, *Neubildung deutschen Bauerntums: Innere Kolonisation im Dritten Reich* (Gesamthochschule Kassel, 1983); Gustavo Corni, *Hitler and the Peasants: Agrarian Policy of the Third Reich, 1930-1939* (New York: Berg, 1990); Daniela Münkel, *Nationalsozialistische Agrarpolitik und Bauernalltag* (Frankfurt: Campus, 1996); Gustavo Corni and Herbert Gies, *Brot-Butter-Kanonen: Die Ernährungswirtschaft in Deutschland unter der Diktatur Hitlers* (Berlin: Akademie, 1997); Christian Böse, *Die Entstehung und Fortbildung des Reichserbhofgesetzes* (Frankfurt: Lang, 2008). An excellent overview in English, with important context on Darré's role in particular, is available in Adam Tooze, "Saving the Peasants" in Tooze, *The Wages of Destruction: The*

Making and Breaking of the Nazi Economy (New York: Viking, 2006), 166-99.

57   Woodruff Smith, *The Ideological Origins of Nazi Imperialism* (Oxford
     University Press, 1996), 243; see also Clifford Lovin, "R. Walther Darré,
     Nazi Agricultural Policy, and Preparation for War" *Occasional Papers
     in German Studies* 7 (1995); Andrea D'Onofrio, "Rassenzucht und
     Lebensraum: Zwei Grundlagen im Blut- und Boden- Gedanken von
     Richard Walther Darré" *Zeitschrift für Geschichtswissenschaft* 49 (2001),
     141-57; and Tooze, *Wages of Destruction*, 198-99. Bramwell's claims along
     these lines, and her approving portrait of the Nazi agricultural minister,
     have nonetheless found fertile ground among other admirers of the
     far right; for an equally naïve view see the entry on Darré by Michael
     Moynihan in Taylor, ed., *Encyclopedia of Religion and Nature*, 450-51.
     Blood and Soil relied centrally and credulously on information supplied
     to Bramwell by Darré's attorney Hans Merkel, himself an anthroposophist
     and veteran promoter of biodynamic agriculture.

58   Citing her own interviews with unnamed "Anthroposophist members of
     Darré's staff" as a source on "relations between followers of Steiner and
     the regime" (Bramwell, *Ecology in the 20th Century*, 270), for example,
     she identified Ludolf Haase and Antony Ludovici as Nazi officials who
     supported biodynamic agriculture. Bramwell appears to have confused J.W.
     Ludowici, a Nazi agricultural specialist, with Anthony Ludovici, a British
     Nazi sympathizer, agrarian ideologue, and admirer of Darré. I have been
     unable to find corroboration for sympathies toward biodynamic agriculture
     on the part of either Haase or Ludowici (the German official), though it is
     always possible that new evidence will come to light. Biodynamic agriculture
     was not, of course, the only variety of organic farming vying for attention
     in Nazi Germany, but it was the most successful. Competing approaches
     included a form of natural farming developed by Hermann Denstädt
     which abjured artificial fertilizers in favor of "living bacterial soil" and had
     the support of Julius Streicher, and the method of "biological cultivation"

promoted by Ewald Könemann in his journal *Bebauet die Erde*.

59 See e.g. Uekoetter, *The Green and the Brown*, 203. Even anarchists have accepted this inaccurate claim at face value; see the review of Uekoetter's book by Jeff Shantz in the *Canadian Journal of History* 43 (2008), 313-14. Uekoetter's recent work is more equivocal on this point; cf. Frank Uekötter, *Die Wahrheit ist auf dem Feld: Eine Wissensgeschichte der deutschen Landwirtschaft* (Göttingen: Vandenhoeck & Ruprecht, 2010), 268-69.

60 Overviews of Darré's thought are available in Clifford Lovin, "Blut und Boden: The Ideological Basis of the Nazi Agricultural Program" *Journal of the History of Ideas* 28 (1967), 279-88; Mathias Eidenbenz, *"Blut und Boden": Zu Funktion und Genese der Metaphern des Agrarismus und Biologismus in der nationalsozialistischen Bauernpropaganda R. W. Darrés* (Frankfurt: Lang, 1993); Frank-Lothar Kroll, *Utopie als Ideologie: Geschichtsdenken und politisches Handeln im Dritten Reich* (Paderborn: Schöningh, 1998), 157-205; D'Onofrio, "Rassenzucht und Lebensraum." For further background on biodynamic agriculture cf. Holger Kirchmann, "Biological Dynamic Farming – An Occult Form of Alternative Agriculture?" *Journal of Agricultural and Environmental Ethics* 7 (1994), 173-87; Zander, *Anthroposophie in Deutschland*, 1579-1607; Reinhard Farkas, "Alternative Landwirtschaft / Biologischer Landbau" in Kerbs and Reulecke, eds., *Handbuch der deutschen Reformbewegungen*, 301-13; Uekötter, *Die Wahrheit ist auf dem Feld*, 232-40 and 413-22. General historical context is available in Gunter Vogt, "The Origins of Organic Farming" in William Lockeretz, ed., *Organic Farming: An International History* (Oxfordshire: CABI, 2007), 9-29.

61 For an account of the steps leadng toward the reversal in Darré's views on biodynamic farming see Georg Halbe, "Bericht über die Entwicklung der Beziehungen zwischen dem Stabsamt des Reichsbauernführers und dem Reichsverband für biologisch-dynamische Wirtschaftsweise" (BAK N1094/II/1), and Erhard Bartsch's June 1941 SD interrogation, BA R58/6223/1: 239

and BA R58/6223/1: 299-305. For Darré's own official version see his June
20, 1940 announcement as Reich Peasant Leader, BA NS 15/304: 57046.

62 See Erhard Bartsch to Alfred Baeumler, January 13, 1939, BA NS 15/304:
57128, as well as Bartsch's 1939 correspondence with Göring's office in BA
R 9349/2.

63 "Um die biologisch-dynamische Düngungsweise: Eine Erklärung des
Reichsernährungsministers" *Die Landware*, January 20, 1940, 2. See also
Darré to Rosenberg, July 24, 1940, BA NS 8/173: 44.

64 Darré to Seifert, May 28, 1941, BAK N1094/II/1. Darré's extremely friendly
1941 correspondence with Seifert shows that by this point both figures
viewed one another as allies in promoting biodynamics. For specific
examples of Darré's wide-ranging efforts on behalf of biodynamics see
the "Geschäftsbericht 1939/40" of the Reichsverband für biologisch-
dynamische Wirtschaftsweise, BA R58/6197/1: 141-43.

65 On Backe see Gesine Gerhard, "Food and Genocide: Nazi Agrarian Politics
in the Occupied Territories of the Soviet Union" *Contemporary European
History* 18 (2009), 45-65; Tooze, *Wages of Destruction*, 538-51; and Christian
Gerlach, *Krieg, Ernährung, Völkermord: Forschungen zur deutschen
Vernichtungspolitik im Zweiten Weltkrieg* (Hamburger Edition, 1998), 13-21
and 189-223. For Backe's vehement opposition to biodynamics see his 1933-
42 correspondence with Darré in BAK N1094/II/20.

66 See e.g. Darré's official statement as Minister of Agriculture from May 19,
1941 in BA NS 26/947, and compare his June 7, 1941 memorandum to his
close collaborators, marked "confidential," in BAK N1094/II/1d.

67 The main association was the *Verein für Bauerntumskunde*, which
campaigned for biodynamic farming from 1939 onward and was re-named
Gesellschaft der Freunde des deutschen Bauerntums in October 1940,
with Darré as president throughout. The association was coordinated
by Wilhelm Kinkelin, Karl August Rust, and Hermann Reischle, all
proponents of organic agriculture. For details see Kinkelin to Reischle,

November 27, 1939, and Rust to Seifert, June 16, 1941, BAK N1094/II/1.
Further biodynamic supporters on Darré's staff included Wilhelm Rauber,
Günther Pacyna, Reinhard Ohnesorge, and Wilhelm Driehaus.

68 Darré, "Anordnung für den persönlichen Stab" June 7, 1941, BAK N1094/II/1d.

69 On Otto Strasser as ecofascist see the entry on him by Patrick Moreau in
Ronald Smelser and Rainer Zitelmann, eds., *Die braune Elite* (Darmstadt:
Wissenschaftliche Buchgesellschaft, 1989), 294-96; for further context
cf. Andrea D'Onofrio, *Ruralismo e storia nel Terzo Reich: Il caso "Odal"*
(Naples: Liguori, 1997); Joshua Hagen, "The Most German of Towns:
Creating an Ideal Nazi Community in Rothenburg ob der Tauber" *Annals
of the Association of American Geographers* 94 (2004), 207-27; Bernhard
Dietz, "Countryside-versus City in European Thought: German and British
Anti-Urbanism between the Wars" *The European Legacy* 13 (2008), 801-14;
Shelley Baranowski, *The Sanctity of Rural Life: Nobility, Protestantism, and
Nazism in Weimar Prussia* (Oxford University Press, 1995). It is important
to keep in mind that the images of the 'peasantry' and 'peasant values'
exalted in the works of Darré and Strasser et al. were ideologies which had
little to do with the actual lives of rural working people but were largely an
invention of disaffected figures from quite different backgrounds projecting
their own longings and resentments onto agrarian contexts.

70 For a representative example see Von Ehrlich, "Bauerntum und
Landschuljahr" *N.S. Lehrerbund Mitteilungsblatt Gau Köln-Aachen*, March
1, 1934, 68-69.

71 Details on Reischle's career can be found in BA SSO/21B: 1020-1137
and BA DS/G131: 2475-2492; for context cf. Heinemann, *Rasse,
Siedlung, deutsches Blut*, 88-89, 114-16, 127-28, 631. His titles included
Hauptamtsleiter im Amt für Agrarpolitik bei der Reichsleitung
der NSDAP, Reichskommissar im Reichsernährungsministerium,
Stabsamtsführer im Reichsnährstand, and Führer im Persönlichen Stab
des Reichsführers-SS. For examples of his publications see Hermann

Reischle, *Reichsbauernführer Darré: Der Kämpfer um Blut und Boden*
(Berlin 1933); Reischle, "Kapitalismus als Nährboden des Judentums"
Odal, January 1937, 530-41; Reischle, "Neubildung deutschen
Bauerntums" *Neues Bauerntum*, June 1939; Reischle, *Nationalsozialistische
Agrarpolitik* (Münster 1941).

72 Merkel's title was Stabshauptabteilungsleiter im Stabsamt des
Reichsbauernführers; in 1935 he was also named Leiter der
Stabshauptabteilung im Reichsnährstand. He initially applied to join
the SS in 1935 but failed the physical examination; he was made an SS
officer in 1936 on special orders from Himmler. For further details see his
handwritten *Lebenslauf* from March 8, 1938 in BA RS/D5477: 311, as well as
his personnel files in BA SSO/310A: 74-114 and BA DS/G179: 2735-2762.

73 In addition to his numerous articles in *Odal: Zeitschrift für Blut und
Boden* see Hans Merkel, "Die Neugestaltung des Wirtschaftsrechts im
Reichsnährstand" *Jahrbuch der nationalsozialistischen Wirtschaft* 1937,
227-37; Merkel, *Agrarpolitik* (Leipzig 1942); Merkel, *Deutsches Bauernrecht*
(Leipzig 1944). The January 1940 issue of *Odal* praised Merkel's analysis of
the changing agricultural situation as Germany defended itself against "the
Jewish-plutocratic war."

74 The voluminous post-war correspondence between Merkel and Darré can be
found in BAK N1094 I/2; Merkel's defense brief and related documents from
Darré's Nuremberg trial are in BAK N1094 I/1. Further details are contained
in an unpublished post-war memoir by Merkel titled "Mein Lebensgang,"
recounting his career during the Third Reich and his role in defending
Darré at Nuremberg. The memoir strongly downplays Merkel's own Nazi
involvement, and many of its claims are controverted by archival evidence. I
am indebted to Ute Merkel for providing a copy of this document.

75 See Halbe's handwritten *Lebenslauf* dated August 14, 1942, BA DS/A97: 660.

76 Georg Halbe, "Lebensgesetzlicher Landbau" *Westermanns Monatshefte*,
November 1940, 128-30; on the book project see Halbe's August 1942

"Verzeichnis umfangreicherer Aufsätze" (BA DS/A97: 664).

77 Cf. Georg Halbe, "Zur neuen Getreideordnung" *Deutschlands Erneuerung*, September 1934, 552-56; Halbe, "Odal, das Lebensgesetz eines ewigen Deutschland" *Odal*, October 1935, 301-06; Halbe, "Goethes Naturanschauung und lebensgesetzlicher Landbau" *Demeter*, December 1940, 116-18; Halbe, "Die Reichsidee" *Leib und Leben*, November 1942, 89-91; Halbe, "Unsterblichkeit" *Leib und Leben*, March 1943, 23; he also published in the *Nationalsozialistische Landpost* and the SS journal *Das schwarze Korps*.

78 Hermann Schneider, *Schicksalsgemeinschaft Europa: Leben und Nahrung aus der europäischen Scholle* (Breslau 1941); see especially 89-102 on biodynamic agriculture.

79 Hermann Schneider to Erhard Bartsch, December 8, 1940, with Schneider's manuscript "Gründung einer europäischen Hauptforschungsstätte für Lebensforschung" (BA R9349/3/Sch); see also Schneider's December 9, 1939 letter to Himmler in the same file, detailing efforts to promote biodynamic farming, as well Schneider's May 19, 1941 letter to Darré containing a four-page clarion call for biodynamics under the title "Stellungnahme zur Frage der naturgesetzlichen Wirtschaftsweise" (BAK N1094/II/1).

80 According to an October 7, 1939 letter from the Wehrwirtschaftsstab beim Oberkommando der Wehrmacht to Reichshauptamtsleiter Rauber, Stabsamt des Reichsbauernführers, the Wehrmacht high command supported "the biodynamic method of cultivation." (BA R58/6223/1: 331) Cf. Erhard Bartsch to Albert Friehe, October 9, 1939, BA R9349/2.

81 Blackbourn, *The Conquest of Nature*, 9. A sophisticated analysis of this ideological convergence can be found in Andrea D'Onofrio, *Razza, sangue e suolo: Utopie della razza e progetti eugenetici nel ruralismo nazista* (Naples: ClioPress, 2007). Cf. Ulrich Linse, *Zurück o Mensch zur Mutter Erde: Landkommunen in Deutschland 1890-1933* (Munich: DTV, 1983),

327-39, and in English see the informative recent study by Corinna Treitel, "Nature and the Nazi Diet" *Food and Foodways* 17 (2009), 139-58.

82   In addition to the figures mentioned here, further supporters of biodynamics such as Karl August Rust and Rudi Peuckert served for years as officials of the SS Office of Race and Settlement.

83   Friehe joined the NSDAP in 1925 and was a candidate for the party in both of the 1932 Reichstag elections; in January 1932 he was appointed 'Fachreferent für bäuerliches Bildungswesen bei der Reichsleitung der NSDAP' and from February 1934 onward he was a 'ständiger Mitarbeiter des Rassenpolitischen Amtes der NSDAP'. Friehe was also 'Leiter der Arbeitsgemeinschaft für biologisch-dynamische Wirtschaftsweise' in Bückeburg in Saxony. Cf. BA PK/A199: 2718, BA PK/C313: 1119-1178, and BA R9349/2/F.

84   See Herman Polzer, "Ein bäuerliches Kulturideal: Zur Jahrestagung für biologisch-dynamische Wirtschaftsweise in Bad Saarow" *Leib und Leben*, February 1939, 29-31, and Bert Becker, *Georg Michaelis: Eine Biographie* (Paderborn: Schöningh, 2007), 667.

85   Kurt Willmann, "Vom Wesen des deutschen Bauerntums" *Demeter*, August 1939, 147.

86   See Erhard Bartsch, "Betriebs-Autarkie" *Demeter*, March 1933, 41-45; Bartsch, *Die biologisch-dynamische Wirtschaftsweise: Überwindung des Materialismus in Landwirtschaft und Gartenbau* (Dresden 1934); Bartsch, "Was ist biologisch-dynamische Wirtschaftsweise?" *Natur und Kultur*, April 1938, 117-18; Herman Polzer, "Reichstagung für biologisch-dynamische Wirtschaftsweise" *Leib und Leben*, January 1936, 18-19. On the growth of the Reich League for Biodynamic Agriculture see the November 1939 audit of the organization, BA R58/6197/1: 40-43; on the degree of Nazi support for the group see the "Geschäftsbericht 1935/36 des Reichsverbandes für biologisch-dynamische Wirtschaftsweise" and the "Geschäftsbericht 1939/40" BA R58/6197/1: 107-09 and 141-43, as well as the report "Tagung

des Reichsverbandes" in *Demeter*, December 1935, 205-06.

87   Cf. Oskar Krüger, "Neue Wege des Landbaues" *Völkischer Beobachter*, August 28, 1940, 7, a lengthy and glowing portrait of biodynamics, particularly Bartsch's estate; Wolfgang Clauß, "Lebensgesetzliche Landbauweise: Eindrücke von einer Besichtigung des Erbhofes Marienhöhe bei Bad Saarow" *Nationalsozialistische Landpost*, July 26, 1940, 3-4; Edmund Sala, "Die Natur als Erzieher" *Die Grüne Post*, November 24, 1940, 6, another fulsome article on biodynamics, pointing especially to the compatibility of organic agriculture with "our National Socialist plans"; and Käthe Wietfeld, "Volkskraft und Volksgesundheit" *Gesundes Leben*, March 1940, 60, which praises the Reich League for Biodynamic Agriculture, Demeter, and Weleda as contributors to the people's health.

88   Franz Zeno Diemer to Hermann Reischle, July 5, 1941, BAK N1094/II/1. Diemer was a Luftwaffe officer and Nazi party official and an avid proponent of biodynamics.

89   See e.g. Erhard Bartsch, "Zurück zum Agrarstaat" *Demeter*, September 1933, 163-64; Bartsch, "Haltet den Boden gesund!" *Demeter*, January 1938, 1; Franz Dreidax, "Heimatpflege und Landwirtschaft" *Demeter*, September 1933, 187-92; "Beitrag zum Autarkieproblem" *Demeter*, August 1933, 139-42; "Kulturschaffendes Bauerntum" *Demeter*, January 1941, 1-2. The journal's subtitle was *Monatsschrift für biologisch-dynamische Wirtschaftsweise*.

90   Ernst Schaaf to Bürgermeister der Stadt Reichenbach, July 6, 1937, BA R9349/1.

91   See *Demeter* July 1940, 64, October 1940, 99, and the opening articles in the September 1939 and 1940 issues.

92   Cf. Max Karl Schwarz, "Bildekräfte im Lebensraum der Landschaft" *Demeter*, April 1939, 59-66; Schwarz, *Zur landschaftlichen Ausgestaltung der Straßen in Norddeutschland* (Berlin: Volk und Reich Verlag, 1940); Erhard Bartsch, "Der Impuls der biologisch-dynamischen

Wirtschaftsweise" *Demeter*, June 1937, 93-95; Franz Dreidax, "Lebendiger Boden – ewiges Volk" *Leib und Leben*, October 1938, 199-205; Dreidax, "Gesundes Brot aus gesundem Boden" *Leib und Leben*, September 1940, 88; Franz Lippert, "Der Bauerngarten" *Leib und Leben*, June 1941, 80-81.

93   The 1938 "Akten-Vermerk für Herrn Hanns Georg Müller" (BA R9349/3/M) blames all the negative aspects of modern agriculture on "Jewish influences" and posits biodynamics as the antidote to such influences, touting *Demeter*'s efforts to counter the harmful effects of the Jews.

94   Erhard Bartsch to Lotar Eickhoff, August 22, 1937, BA R9349/2.

95   On Müller see Bothe, *Neue Deutsche Heilkunde 1933–1945*, 217-27; Fritzen, *Gesünder Leben*, 64-77 and 93-103; and Müller's own 1975 affidavit in Gilbhard, *Die Thule-Gesellschaft*, 243-47. On his extremely enthusiastic support for biodynamics see the minutes of Müller's May 14, 1939 meeting with biodynamic leaders in BA R 9349/2.

96   See the 1938 correspondence between Müller and the Reichsverband für biologisch-dynamische Wirtschaftsweise in BA R9349/1; Müller also intervened with the national association of grain producers and the Reich Commissar for Price Regulation, among many others. Müller headed the *Lebensreform* bureau in the *Sachverständigenbeirat für Volksgesundheit*, part of the NSDAP *Reichsleitung*, acting as a loyal and enthusiastic ally of biodynamic concerns. The correspondence between Müller and the Reich League for Biodynamic Agriculture extends from 1934 to 1940. See also the numerous letters from Bartsch to Müller in BA R9349/3/M.

97   Müller's publishing house, the Müllersche Verlagshandlung, produced works by anthroposophist, *völkisch*, organic, and environmentalist authors before, during, and after the Nazi era. Its biodynamic publications include Franz Dreidax, *Das Bauen im Lebendigen: Eine Einführung in die biologisch-dynamische Wirtschaftsweise* (1939); Max Karl Schwarz, *Obstbau unter Berücksichtigung der biologisch-dynamischen Wirtschaftsweise* (1939); Franz Lippert, *Zur Praxis des Heilpflanzenbaus* (1939); Nicolaus Remer,

Gesundheit und Leistung bei Haustieren (1940); Hellmut Bartsch and Franz Dreidax, *Der lebendige Dünger* (1941). Pro-biodynamic articles by leading Nazi *Lebensreform* advocates such as Herman Polzer, Eva Hauck and Fritz Hugo Hoffmann appeared regularly in *Leib und Leben: Zeitschrift der Reformbewegung*, edited and published by Müller.

98 See e.g. Robert Banfield, "Landwirtschaftliche Tagung für biologisch-dynamische Wirtschaftsweise," *Leib und Leben*, January 1935, 17-19. Banfield was deputy director of the *Deutsche Gesellschaft für Lebensreform*.

99 Bartsch's and Dreidax's colleague Herman Polzer described the *Deutsche Gesellschaft für Lebensreform* thus: "Our Society is not a bourgeois association but a working group of active National Socialists. The bedrock on which we build is the National Socialist worldview. Every one of us recognizes its laws of life as our foundation and our binding duty, not only politically but in our entire personal and daily life." (*Leib und Leben*, May 1941, 72) The organization comprised groups dedicated to alternative health, nutrition, farming, and other versions of 'lifestyle reform' as part of the Nazi project. Cf. Franz Dreidax, "Jahrestagung der Lebensreform in Innsbruck August 1938," *Demeter*, October 1938, 178-79.

100 See e.g. Wilhelm Rauber, "Bauern 'kraft Gesetzes' oder wesenhaftes Bauerntum? Gedanken über die Notwendigkeit eines lebensgesetzlichen Landbaus," *Nationalsozialistische Monatshefte*, November 1940, 676-82; Erhard Bartsch, "Vom Wesen des Betriebsorganismus," *Odal*, April 1940, 287-90; Bartsch, "Der Erbhof Marienhöhe: Ein Beispiel lebensgesetzlicher Landbauweise," *Odal*, September 1940, 695-701.

101 BA R58/6223/1: 320; BA RK/I18: 11914 and 2104; BA RK/I85: 1990. Darré also honored Bartsch's biodynamic estate with the official designation of "model farm."

102 Cf. Bartsch's 1939-1940 correspondence with Ilse Hess, wife of Rudolf Hess, BA R9349/2/H; Rudolf Hess to Alwin Seifert, November 14, 1938, BA R58/6223/1: 318; Reischle to Keitel, October 25, 1940, BA R58/6223/1:

328. Ilse Hess was a member of the Society for the Promotion of Biodynamic Agriculture.

103 December 1934 'Geschäftsbericht des Reichsverbandes für biologisch-dynamische Wirtschaftsweise' in BA R58/6197/1: 192; Seifert to Lippert, October 13, 1937, BA R9349/3/S; Wilhelm zur Linden, *Blick durchs Prisma* (Frankfurt: Klostermann, 1965), 247.

104 July 6, 1941 SD report on the Reichsverband für biologisch-dynamische Wirtschaftsweise, BA R58/6223/1: 242.

105 For examples see the December 19, 1939 memorandum by Nicolaus Remer of the Reich League for Biodynamic Agriculture, and Hermann Schneider to Heinrich Himmler, December 9, 1939, both in BA R9349/3; the May 9, 1940 report by Heinrich Vogel on biodynamics and SS 'settlements', BA NS3/1175; Bartsch to Hess, November 9, 1940, BA R58/6223/1: 310; and Fritz Hoffmann, "Lebensgesetzliche Grundlagen" *Leib und Leben*, November 1940, 109-10.

106 Pancke to Himmler, November 20, 1939, BA NS2/60: 51-59.

107 Himmler to Pohl, June 18, 1941, BA NS19/3122: 83; Brandt to Vogel, March 2, 1942, BA NS19/3122: 38.

108 Pancke to Pohl, February 29, 1940, BA PK/A199: 2778; Pancke to Heydrich, January 8, 1940, BA PK/A199: 2780; and Pancke's further correspondence in support of biodynamics as head of the SS Office of Race and Settlement in the same file.

109 Pohl to Himmler, June 17, 1940, BA NS19/3122: 80.

110 Bernhard Strebel, *Das KZ Ravensbrück: Geschichte eines Lagerkomplexes* (Paderborn: Schöningh, 2003), 212-13. Extensive information on SS biodynamic plantations is available in Enno Georg, *Die wirtschaftlichen Unternehmungen der SS* (Stuttgart: Deutsche Verlags-Anstalt, 1963), 62-66; Hermann Kaienburg, *Die Wirtschaft der SS* (Berlin: Metropol, 2003), 771-855; and Wolfgang Jacobeit and Christoph Kopke, *Die Biologisch-dynamische Wirtschaftsweise im KZ: Die Güter der 'Deutschen*

Versuchsanstalt für Ernährung und Verpflegung' der SS von 1939 bis 1945
(Berlin: Trafo, 1999).

111 BA R58/6197/1: 162.

112 BA NS3/1430: 114; BA SM/L40: 623-630. For details on the Dachau
biodynamic plantation cf. Robert Sigel, "Heilkräuterkulturen im KZ: Die
Plantage in Dachau" *Dachauer Hefte* 4 (1988), 164-73; Walter Wuttke-
Groneberg, "Die Heilkräuterplantage im KZ Dachau" in Gerhard
Baader, ed., *Medizin und Nationalsozialismus* (Berlin: Verlagsgesellschaft
Gesundheit, 1980), 116-20; Daniella Seidl, *"Zwischen Himmel und Hölle":
Das Kommando 'Plantage' des Konzentrationslagers Dachau* (Munich: Utz,
2008). According to a December 1939 DVA report, the Dachau plantation
was built by camp inmates, "mainly Jews and Gypsies" (BA NS3/1433: 133).

113 Franz Lippert, *Das Wichtigste in Kürze über Kräuter und Gewürze* (Berlin:
Nordland Verlag, 1943). Nordland Verlag was the SS publishing house. On
Seifert's role at the Dachau plantation and his relationship with Lippert see
Seidl, *"Zwischen Himmel und Hölle"*, 156-57.

114 Although estranged from his father, longtime anthroposophist and Nazi
party member Hanns Rascher, Sigmund Rascher maintained very friendly
relations with leading figures in the biodynamic movement, including
Otto Lerchenfeld, Ehrenfried Pfeiffer, and Franz Lippert. He published
an article on biodynamics in 1936 and recommended biodynamic
literature to Himmler. Substantial material on Rascher can be found in BA
NS21/921a, BA NS21/915, BA NS21/916, and BA NS21/925.

115 See the memo on "Siedler für den Osten" in BA NS3/1175: 57, and Seifert
to Bodenstedt, April 2, 1941, BAK N1094/II/1.

116 March 1941 DVA report, BA R58/6223/1: 365.

117 Vogel to Brandt, Persönlicher Stab Reichsführer-SS, October 29, 1943,
BA NS19/3122: 27-28. Grund was one of the foremost spokesmen for
biodynamic agriculture in Nazi Germany. He joined the NSDAP in May
1933 and the SA in November 1933. In August 1942 he was named an SS-

Untersturmführer and in July 1943 was promoted to Obersturmführer; his SS
title was 'Referent für landwirtschaftliche Fragen' (BA SSO/40A: 853-871).

118 Vogel to Brandt, May 15, 1943, "Betrifft: Prüfung des naturgemäßen
Landbaues (früher biologisch-dynamische Wirtschaftsweise)" BA
NS19/3122: 35.

119 Even anthroposophist accounts note the considerable increase in
biodynamic production during the Nazi era. Wilhelm zur Linden,
chairman of the Society for the Promotion of Biodynamic Agriculture and
a close associate of Bartsch, claims that there were 2000 biodynamic farms
and gardens in Germany by 1940 (zur Linden, *Blick durchs Prisma*, 247).
Such figures are difficult to verify with precision, but the basic thrust is
confirmed by archival evidence; the annual reports of the *Reichsverband
für biologisch-dynamische Wirtschaftsweise* indicate a steady rise in activity
and confidence from 1933 onward.

120 The fact that the biodynamic movement influenced Nazi agricultural
policy has, after all, been recognized in mainstream scholarship for some
time. For one example see Judith Baumgartner, *Ernährungsreform -
Antwort auf Industrialisierung und Ernährungswandel* (Frankfurt: Lang,
1992), 55-57. Baumgartner's treatment is by no means aggressively critical;
her brief overview of the role of biodynamics in helping to shape the Third
Reich's agrarian practices is measured and matter-of-fact. A much more
detailed account can be found in Gunter Vogt's 2000 study *Entstehung
und Entwicklung des ökologischen Landbaus im deutschsprachigen Raum*
and in Vogt, "Ökologischer Landbau im Dritten Reich" *Zeitschrift für
Agrargeschichte und Agrarsoziologie* 48 (2000), 161-80. For an extended
discussion in English see Treitel, "Nature and the Nazi Diet," 148-54.
Treitel relies uncritically on apologetic anthroposophist accounts, but
raises many important issues and provides crucial historical context.
Her conclusion observes: "the Nazi case draws attention to the political
promiscuity of natural foods and farming in the twentieth century. Today,

when these practices seem to belong so clearly to the progressive left, it strikes us as oddly perverse that at midcentury they were associated with the militaristic right. These links, however, are neither strange anomalies nor historical relics." (154)

121 For a paradigmatic example see Avner de-Shalit, "Ruralism or Environmentalism?" *Environmental Values* 5 (1996), 47-58. De-Shalit's political perspectives are often admirable, but his idealist account ignores the longstanding historical convergence of ruralism and environmentalism as well as right-wing authoritarianism and ecological politics.

122 Sax, *Animals in the Third Reich*, 43.

123 Pois, *National Socialism and the Religion of Nature*, 127. Background on the role of agrarian ideologies in justifying genocide is available in Ben Kiernan, *Blood and Soil: A World History of Genocide and Extermination from Sparta to Darfur* (Yale University Press, 2007). For a recent thoughtful reflection on this issue see Boaz Neumann, "National Socialism, Holocaust, and Ecology" in Dan Stone, ed., *The Holocaust and Historical Methodology* (Oxford: Berghahn, forthcoming 2011).

124 Thomas Lekan, "Regionalism and the Politics of Landscape Preservation in the Third Reich" *Environmental History* 4 (1999), 399.

125 This convoluted history raises the vexed question of modernity, a factor which inevitably complicates historical and political discussion of the themes treated here. Many recent commentators have taken previous generations of scholars to task for positing a simplistic schema of anti-modern sentiment as one of the chief roots of National Socialism. In my view, this is a foreshortened reading of the work of George Mosse and Fritz Stern et al.; for all their shortcomings, the earlier studies by Mosse and Stern traced an important intellectual lineage which newer analyses would do well to recognize and take into account. The distinctively modern character of much of right-wing ecology does not somehow render this tradition more palatable. At the same time, rejecting modernity itself as

hopelessly compromised by its worst features is a foolish form of defeatism. A more reasonable radical position would be to affirm the emancipatory strivings which underlie the modern project precisely by combating the distorted forms modernity has taken: capitalism, the nation-state, reified science and technology, and so forth. What much of contemporary 'radical environmentalism' does, rather, is to condemn modernity as a whole and thus bury its latent liberatory potential while leaving its present concrete manifestations unchallenged. The dream of reactionary ecology is to escape history; an informed and aware radical ecology seeks to re-shape history.

126 Landry, "How Brown were the Conservationists," 91.

127 Similar objections have been raised in Germany by scholars as well as activists. For penetrating analyses see Joachim Wolschke-Bulmahn, "Zu Verdrängungs- und Verschleierungstendenzen in der Geschichtsschreibung des Naturschutzes in Deutschland" in Uwe Schneider and Joachim Wolschke-Bulmahn, eds., *Gegen den Strom: Gert Gröning zum 60. Geburtstag* (Universität Hannover, 2004), 313-35; Wolschke-Bulmahn, "Naturschutz und Nationalsozialismus - Darstellungen im Spannungsfeld von Verdrängung, Verharmlosung und Interpretation" in Gert Gröning and Joachim Wolschke-Bulmahn, eds., *Naturschutz und Demokratie!?* (Munich: Meidenbauer, 2006), 91-114; Peter Bierl and Clemens Heni, "Eine deutsche Liebe: Über die braunen Wurzeln der Grünen und die Lücken der Naturschutzforschung" *Konkret*, January 2008, 24-26. In English see the pioneering argument by Douglas Weiner, "Demythologizing Environmentalism" *Journal of the History of Biology* 25 (1992), 385-411. Weiner takes right-wing ecology seriously as a historical phenomenon and a political challenge, and emphasizes the political nature of all environmental visions.

128 Aside from the anti-humanism that remains a prominent feature of current environmental thought, questions along these lines need to be raised even when they are bound to step on some toes. To choose merely one example:

What role does the notion of natural 'purity' play in contemporary practices like organic farming or veganism or wilderness protection? Does the fact that fascists sometimes embraced related practices call for reflection on their political resonance? Neither simple condemnation nor simple dismissal does justice to such complex dilemmas. For a critical appraisal of the aporias of "romantic ecology" see Chaia Heller, "Rescuing Lady Nature: Ecology and the Cult of the Romantic" in Heller, *Ecology of Everyday Life* (Montreal: Black Rose, 1999), 13-38.

129 On this point see the fine recent study by Noel Sturgeon, *Environmentalism in Popular Culture: Gender, Race, Sexuality, and the Politics of the Natural* (University of Arizona Press, 2009), 8-14, classifying biocentric approaches as part of mainstream environmentalism rather than radical ecological politics. Sturgeon writes: "conceiving of nature and culture as radically separate spheres, presenting humans as a universalized cause of damage to a pristine nonhuman environment, and promoting individualistic solutions to environmental problems without considering the need for structural, economic, or social change does not get at the root of our problems." (8)

130 For an example of these overstated apprehensions in a German context see the comparison between the Nazis and the Greens in Götz Warnke, *Die grüne Ideologie: Heile-Welt-Mythen, Gesellschaftsutopien und Naturromantik als Ausdruck einer angstbestimmten Politik* (Frankfurt: Lang, 1998), 446-47.